Really learn

100

phrasal verbs

OXFORD

UNIVERSITY PRESS

OXFORD
UNIVERSITY PRESS

Great Clarendon Street, Oxford OX2 6DP

Oxford University Press is a department of the University of Oxford.
It furthers the University's objective of excellence in research, scholarship,
and education by publishing worldwide in

Oxford New York

Auckland Cape Town Dar es Salaam Hong Kong Karachi
Kuala Lumpur Madrid Melbourne Mexico City Nairobi
New Delhi Shanghai Taipei Toronto

With offices in

Argentina Austria Brazil Chile Czech Republic France Greece
Guatemala Hungary Italy Japan Poland Portugal Singapore
South Korea Switzerland Thailand Turkey Ukraine Vietnam

OXFORD and OXFORD ENGLISH are registered trade marks of
Oxford University Press in the UK and in certain other countries

ISBN-13: 978 0 19 431583 8
ISBN-10: 0 19 431583 5

Designer: Christopher Howson, Howson Baxter Design
Cover: Richard Morris, Stonesfield Design

Text capture and typesetting by Oxford University Press

Printed in China

Contents

HOW TO ... REALLY LEARN PHRASAL VERBS

This book covers 100 of the most frequent and useful phrasal verbs in English, with their main meanings. You may find that a phrasal verb has other meanings that are not covered in this book, but our aim is to give you what you need to master the phrasal verbs that you need in everyday English.

The phrasal verbs in this book are arranged in alphabetical order according to the particles, so that *look after* comes before *bring up*, but you can do the pages in any order, as each page deals with a separate verb. There are also ten revision pages, which bring together verbs that have been covered in the other pages.

The TITLE of each page shows you the general form of the phrasal verb. This already gives you some grammatical information - notice how this particular verb can be used both with and without an object, and how the object must be 'somebody' (i.e. a person).

> ## WAKE UP; WAKE *somebody* UP

STUDY is a very important section, which you should read carefully. These sentences show you what context the phrasal verb is usually used in and the most common ways it is used. All possible grammar patterns are shown in this section. You should keep referring back to this section to help you complete the other sections.

> **STUDY** Read these sentences carefully.
>
> • He's always in a bad mood when he **wakes up**.
> • Please try not to **wake** the baby **up**. I've only just got him to sleep.
> • Sh! You'll **wake up** the whole family if you don't keep quiet.
> • Will you **wake** me **up** at 7 o'clock tomorrow, please?
> • We **were woken up** by the sound of breaking glass.

CHECK
MEANING
Remember to look back at the example sentences to help you work out the meaning from context.

GRAMMAR
In this section you must decide which of the sentences are grammatically correct. This will show you which grammar patterns are possible with the phrasal verb. Remember, all the possible grammar patterns are used in the **STUDY** section. In this section you can circle the answers or use a tick (✓) or a cross (✗).

> **CHECK** Use the sentences in the Study box to help you do these exercises.
>
> *MEANING*
> **What is the opposite of *wake up*? Choose <u>one</u> answer.**
> **a)** get out of bed   **b)** lie down   **c)** go to sleep
>
> *GRAMMAR*
> **Which of these are grammatically possible?**
> **a)** She woke up.
> **b)** She woke her father up.
> **c)** She woke up her father.
> **d)** She woke him up.
> **e)** She woke up him.
> **f)** He was woken up.

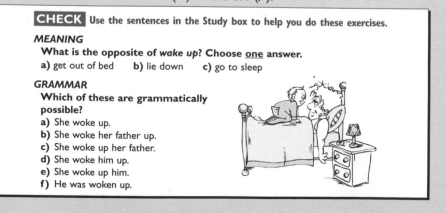

Make sure you check your answers to the *MEANING* and *GRAMMAR* exercises before you move on to the **PRACTISE** section.

In the **PRACTISE** section, there are one or two exercises that enable you to practise using what you have learned and that get you using the phrasal verb in a natural way. If you have difficulty, look back at the **STUDY** and the **CHECK** sections to help you. Again, you should check your answers carefully after you have completed the tasks.

PRACTISE

1 **Respond to the following in an appropriate way, using the verb** *wake up* **or** *wake somebody up* **in each case:**
   a) Did you sleep well last night?
      No, I ....
   b) Is Dad still in bed?
      Yes. Don't ....

2 **Are the following sentences grammatically correct? Correct any errors that you find.**
   a) It's 8 o'clock. Shall I wake Sarah up now?
   b) Why do you always wake up me when you come home? Can't you be quieter?
   c) She was waked up three times during the night by the noise outside.

Now check your answers by looking at *wake up; wake sb up* **on p. 101.**

The **BUILD YOUR VOCABULARY** section gives extra information about the phrasal verb if it is important or particularly useful. For **WAKE UP** you are given information on *RELATED WORDS*. This tells you if there is a noun or an adjective that is derived from the phrasal verb.

BUILD YOUR VOCABULARY

RELATED WORDS
adjective. **wake-up** *(This is only used before a noun.)*
A telephone call that is intended to wake you up is a **wake-up call**.

Other information that you will find in this section on other pages includes:

OTHER MEANINGS:
This tells you if the phrasal verb can be used with a related meaning or another common meaning that will be useful for you.

SYNONYMS:
This shows you common phrasal verbs or single-word verbs that are used with the same meaning.

OPPOSITES:
This tells you if there is a phrasal verb that is used with the opposite meaning.

SIMILAR VERBS:
This tells you about other phrasal verbs that are similar in meaning or in use.

REVIEW PAGES
These pages in the middle of the book look at the meanings of some of the particles used with phrasal verbs and help you test your knowledge of the verbs you have studied in this book.

COME ACROSS *somebody or something*

- While she was cleaning, she **came across** a pair of gold earrings.
- I've never **come across** anything like this before. What is it?
- Whose book is this? I **came across** it in a drawer.
- She is the most difficult woman I have ever **come across**.

CHECK Use the sentences in the Study box to help you do these exercises.

MEANING

1 Complete the meaning of *come across somebody or something* by putting the words below into the correct place:

chance   planned   meet

to find or .... somebody or something by ....,
without having .... or thought about it

2 If you *come across* a book in a bookshop, which of the following might be true?
  a) You didn't know it was there.
  b) Your teacher had told you to go to the bookshop and buy it.

GRAMMAR

Which of these are grammatically possible?
  a) She came a book across.
  b) She came across a book.
  c) She came it across.
  d) She came across it.

Now check your answers by looking at *come across sb/sth* on p. 102.

PRACTISE

There is one grammatical error in each of the following sentences. Can you find and correct it?
  a) Did you came across anything interesting during your investigation?
  b) This is an unusual book. My father came it across in the library.
  c) This is a recipe that I came across it in a French dictionary of cooking.
  d) James is the strangest person I've ever coming across!
  e) Have you come a girl across called Maisy White on your course?
Now check your answers by looking at *come across sb/sth* on p. 102.

BUILD YOUR VOCABULARY

SYNONYMS

The verb **come across somebody** can be replaced by **bump into somebody**, meaning 'to meet somebody by chance':
I came across/bumped into an old school friend the other day in a bookshop.

LOOK AFTER *somebody, something or yourself*

- She found that **looking after** two young children on her own was not easy.
- Who's **looking after** the apartment while Amy and Ben are away?
- That bike was expensive. You should **look after** it.
- He was sixteen, and he felt that he was old enough to **look after** himself.
- My sister is still very ill and is **being looked after** by our parents.

CHECK Use the sentences in the Study box to help you do these exercises.

MEANING

Choose the best answer to complete each part of this meaning of *look after somebody or something*:

a) not alone   **b)** dry   **c)** safe   **d)** happy   **e)** in good condition

If you look after somebody you make sure that they are............................ *Condition*

If you look after something you make sure that it is..............

GRAMMAR

Which of these are grammatically possible?

a) I looked my brother after.
b) I looked after my brother.
c) I looked him after.
d) I looked after him.
e) My brother was looked after.

Now check your answers by looking at *look after sb/sth/yourself* on p. 106.

PRACTISE

Complete the following sentences using the correct form of *look after* and one of the objects below:

himself   him   children   your clothes

a) When he was in hospital, the nurses .... very well.
b) Stop worrying about Tom! He's quite old enough to ....
c) You can always ask Kath to babysit. She loves ....
d) Your new coat is dirty already! I wish you would ....

Now check your answers by looking at *look after sb/sth/yourself* on p. 106.

BUILD YOUR VOCABULARY

SYNONYMS

Care for and **take care of** mean the same as **look after**. **Care for** is more formal. **Look after** is used more in British English and **take care of** in American English.

*She has a new job, **caring for** elderly patients.*
*When his wife got sick, he left work so that he could **take care of** her.*

2

TAKE AFTER *somebody*

STUDY Read these sentences carefully.

- I **take after** my mother in looks, but people say I've got my father's character.
- He's very musical. He **takes after** his grandfather in that respect.
- Who do you **take after** - your mother or your father?
- Jack doesn't **take after** his father at all.

CHECK Use the sentences in the Study box to help you do these exercises.

MEANING

To *take after somebody* means 'to look like or behave like an older member of your family'. Which of these people can you *take after*?

a) your son   **b)** your father   **c)** your younger sister
d) your grandmother   **e)** your aunt   **f)** your friend

GRAMMAR

Which of these are grammatically possible?
a) He takes his mother after.
b) He takes after his mother.
c) He takes her after.
d) He takes after her.
e) He is taken after.

      Now check your answers by looking at *take after sb* **on p. 108.**

PRACTISE

1 Match the two halves to make complete sentences:

a) I take after my mother	**i)** as we are both very impatient.
b) I don't think I take after	**ii)** because I've got green eyes like her.
c) I am told I take after my father	**iii)** but I don't think we are very similar.
d) My father and I both love climbing	**iv)** my mother or my father.
e) I must take after my grandfather	**v)** so I take after him in that respect.

2 Who do <u>you</u> take after? Write some sentences about yourself, using the verb *take after*. Use the complete sentences from the last exercise as examples to follow.

    ....

    ....

    ....

    Now check your answers by looking at *take after sb* **on p. 108.**

GIVE something AWAY

- I can't believe you just **gave** those tickets **away**!
- The magazine is **giving away** six luxury holidays this month.
- The old computer still works. Shall we sell it or **give** it **away**?
- Over one million dollars has **been given away** since the TV show began.

CHECK Use the sentences in the Study box to help you do these exercises.

MEANING

Use one of the phrases below to complete the explanation of this meaning of *give something away*:

to give something to somebody ...

a) because it is old and broken
b) in exchange for something else
c) as a gift

GRAMMAR

Which of these are grammatically possible?

a) She gave her clothes away.
b) She gave away her clothes.
c) She gave them away.
d) She gave away them.
e) They were given away.

Now check your answers by looking at *give sth away* on p. 104.

PRACTISE

Complete these sentences with the correct form of *give something away* **and one of the words or phrases below:**

his old car   all his money   everything   them   the rest

a) Dave has decided to _Give_ ~~all his money away~~ to charity.
b) Do you want one of these bananas? They were _giving them away_
   free at the market.
c) I had lots of spare tickets, so I sold four of them and _give the rest away_
d) He's very generous - he _gave his old car_ when he bought the new one.
e) I don't need this stuff. I've decided to _give everything away_.

Now check your answers by looking at *give sth away* on p. 104.

BUILD YOUR VOCABULARY

RELATED WORDS

noun: **a giveaway**
We're offering 15 lucky readers five CDs in our great CD **giveaway**.
adjective: **give-away** *(This is only used before a noun.)*
The shop is closing down, so it's selling everything at **give-away** *(= very low)* **prices**.

PUT something AWAY

STUDY **Read these sentences carefully.**

- When the bell rang, the students quickly **put** their books **away**.
- He always **puts away** his toys when he's finished playing with them.
- I carefully folded all my winter clothes and **put** them **away** in the cupboard.
- To her surprise, she found that all the dishes had **been** washed and **put away**.

CHECK **Use the sentences in the Study box to help you do these exercises.**

MEANING

Choose the best meaning for this use of *put something away*:
- **a)** to put something far away from you because you do not want it near you
- **b)** to put something in a bin or trash can because you do not want it
- **c)** to put something in a box, a drawer, etc. because you have finished using it

GRAMMAR

Which of these are grammatically possible?
- **a)** He put his things away.
- **b)** He put away his things.
- **c)** He put them away.
- **d)** He put away them.
- **e)** His things were put away.

Now check your answers by looking at *put sth away* on p. 107.

PRACTISE

1 Complete these sentences with the correct form of *put away* and one of the objects below:

them   your toys   it   the cakes   the car

- **a)** You'd better _put the cakes away_ before I eat them all!
- **b)** Do you want to listen to this CD again or shall I _put it away_ ?
- **c)** Stop playing and _put your toys away_ now, Tim. It's time for bed.
- **d)** I think I'll _put the car away_ in the garage - it's safer than leaving it in the street.
- **e)** Why do you always leave your clothes on the floor? Why can't you _put your them away_.

2 Answer these questions in any way you like, using the verb *put something away*:
- **a)** Have you finished with the dictionary?
  I already put it away
- **b)** Where's the milk?
  I put it away in the fridge

Now check your answers by looking at *put sth away* on p. 107.

THROW something AWAY

STUDY Read these sentences carefully.

- She **threw** the letter **away** without reading it.
- Every year the average family **throws away** two tonnes of waste.
- Our old computer's completely useless now. We'll have to **throw** it **away**.
- All the fruit had gone bad and had to **be thrown away**.

CHECK Use the sentences in the Study box to help you do these exercises.

MEANING

If you *throw something away*, what do you do? Choose <u>one</u> answer.
- **a)** You put it in a safe place because it is very important.
- **b)** You put it in a rubbish bin or trash can because you do not want it.
- **c)** You put it somewhere quickly to look at later.

GRAMMAR

Which of these are grammatically possible?
- **a)** She threw the jacket away.
- **b)** She threw away the jacket.
- **c)** She threw it away.
- **d)** She threw away it.
- **e)** The jacket was thrown away.

Now check your answers by looking at *throw sth away* on p. 109.

PRACTISE

Respond to the following using *throw something away* in an appropriate form. The first one has been done for you as an example.
- **a)** This pen doesn't work any more.
  Throw it away then.
- **b)** These boots are falling apart. I can't wear them any more.
  ....
- **c)** Do you want to keep yesterday's newspaper?
  I'm going to recycle it, so don't ....
- **d)** What shall I do with this old shirt and tie?
  You can keep the shirt, but ....

Now check your answers by looking at *throw sth away* on p. 109.

BUILD YOUR VOCABULARY

RELATED WORDS

adjective: **throwaway** *(This is only used before a noun.)*
A **throwaway razor** is one that is intended to be used only once or for a very short time before you get rid of it.

SYNONYMS

The verb **throw something out** has the same meaning.

CALL BACK; CALL *somebody* BACK

STUDY Read these sentences carefully.

- I'm afraid Mr. Smith is in a meeting. Can you **call back** later?
- There's a phone message for you: can you **call** John **back** this evening?
- I left lots of messages for Sue, but she never **called** me **back**.

CHECK Use the sentences in the Study box to help you do these exercises.

MEANING

<u>Two</u> of the sentences below are correct explanations of this meaning of
call (somebody) back. Which one is <u>not</u> correct?
a) to telephone somebody again
b) to telephone somebody
c) to telephone somebody who telephoned you earlier

GRAMMAR

Which of these are grammatically possible?
a) I called back later.
b) I called my parents back later.
c) I called back my parents later.
d) I called them back later.
e) I called back them later.

Now check your answers by looking at *call back; call sb back* on p. 101.

PRACTISE

Complete these sentences in an appropriate way, using a form of *call
back* or *call somebody back* and anything else the sentence needs:
a) She wasn't in when I phoned the first time, so I ....
b) I'm rather busy at the moment, Sam. Can I ....?
c) I left a message with his secretary and he ....
d) I've phoned her three times today, but she ....

Now check your answers by looking at *call back; call sb back* on p. 101.

BUILD YOUR VOCABULARY

RELATED WORDS

noun: **a callback**
This noun has two meanings: **1** a device in a telephone that automatically calls
again the number that was busy when you first called it: *a **callback** facility*
2 a telephone call that you make to somebody who has called you earlier:
*Please leave your name and number and we will give you a **callback**.*

SIMILAR VERBS

You can use other verbs instead of **call**, especially in British English:
*I'll **ring** / **phone** you **back** with the details later.*

7

BREAK DOWN

STUDY Read these sentences carefully.

- Why are you late? Did the bus **break down**?
- What a terrible journey! We **broke down** twice on the way home.
- I'm nervous about using the washing machine in case it **breaks down** again.

CHECK Use the sentences in the Study box to help you do these exercises.

MEANING

Break down means 'to stop working because of a fault'. What <u>type</u> of things can *break down*? Choose <u>two</u> of the following:

a) tools   **b)** machines   **c)** vehicles

GRAMMAR

Which of these are grammatically possible?

a) We broke down.
b) We broke down the car.
c) The car broke down.
d) The car broke itself down.

Now check your answers by looking at *break down* on p. 101.

PRACTISE

1 *Break* or *break down*? Choose the best alternative. Use the answers to the **MEANING** exercise to help you.

a) Can I borrow your pen? Mine's ***broken/broken down***.
b) If the air conditioning system ***breaks/breaks down***, call the engineer.
c) I tried to cut some very thick paper and the scissors ***broke/broke down***.
d) 'My new mobile phone's ***broken/broken down***.' 'Did you drop it again?'

2 Answer the following questions, using the verb *break down*:

a) Why are you washing your clothes by hand?

   Because ....

b) Is your car reliable?

   Yes, ...

Now check your answers by looking at *break down* on p. 101.

BUILD YOUR VOCABULARY

RELATED WORDS

noun: **a breakdown**
We had a **breakdown** on the way home.
adjective: **broken-down** *(This is usually used before a noun.)*
a **broken-down** car
These words are usually used about cars.

CUT DOWN

STUDY Read these sentences carefully.

- Even if you've smoked all your life, it's never too late to **cut down** or stop.
- I've spent far too much money this month - I really must **cut down**.
- If you want to lose weight, try **cutting down** on fatty snacks such as crisps.

CHECK Use the sentences in the Study box to help you do these exercises.

MEANING
Use <u>two</u> of the words below to complete this meaning of *cut down*:

more   less   change   improve

to eat, drink or use .... of something, usually
to .... your health or your situation

GRAMMAR
Which of these are grammatically possible?
a) I cut down.
b) I cut down unhealthy food.
c) I cut down on unhealthy food.

Now check your answers by looking at *cut down* on p. 102.

PRACTISE

1 Your friend wants to lose weight and get fit. Write some advice to him/her, using *cut down (on something)*:

....

....

2 Are <u>you</u> trying to *cut down* on anything? Is there anything that you think you should *cut down on*?

....

....

Now check your answers by looking at *cut down* on p. 102.

BUILD YOUR VOCABULARY

SYNONYMS
Cut back (on something) is also used with this meaning, especially in American English:
*The doctor's told me to **cut back on** red meat.*

SIMILAR VERBS
Give up means 'to stop doing or having something completely'. Look at these examples:
*My doctor has advised me to **cut down on** alcohol* (= drink less alcohol).
*My doctor says I have to **give up** alcohol* (= stop drinking alcohol).

9

LET *somebody* DOWN

> **STUDY** Read these sentences carefully.
>
> • When he missed that penalty, he felt that he'd **let** the team **down**.
> • We think that this government has **let down** particular communities.
> • Don't worry - I won't **let** you **down** this time, I promise.
> • He finds it hard to trust anyone - he's **been** badly **let down** in the past.

CHECK Use the sentences in the Study box to help you do these exercises.

MEANING

When somebody *lets you down*, you feel disappointed. Why do you feel this way? Choose <u>one</u> answer.

a) somebody has failed to help or support you in the way that you hoped or expected

b) you wanted to help or support somebody but they didn't want you to

GRAMMAR

Which of the following are grammatically possible?

a) He let his parents down.
b) He let down his parents.
c) He let them down.
d) He let down them.
e) They were let down.

Now check your answers by looking at *let sb down* on p. 106.

PRACTISE

1 Your friend has promised to take you out for a meal on your birthday, but she *lets you down*. What does she do? Choose the best answer.

a) She has to work a bit late and changes the appointment to one hour later.
b) She forgets and doesn't arrive at all.
c) She takes you to a fast food restaurant.

2 Rewrite the following sentences so that the meaning stays the same, using a form of *let somebody down*:

a) If he promises that he'll do something for somebody, he always does it.
   He never ....

b) If I don't pass these exams, I'll feel that I've disappointed my parents.
   If I fail, I'll feel ....

Now check your answers by looking at *let sb down* on p. 106.

BUILD YOUR VOCABULARY

RELATED WORDS

noun: **a let-down** (= something that is not as good as you thought or hoped it would be)
*I enjoyed the movie but I thought the ending was rather a **let-down**.*

PUT *somebody or something* DOWN

STUDY Read these sentences carefully.

- She's always **putting** her glasses **down** somewhere and losing them.
- At the end of the exam the teacher told everyone to **put down** their pens.
- You're going to break that vase if you're not careful. **Put** it **down**.
- **Put** me **down**, Mummy!
- He heard the sound of the phone **being put down**.

CHECK Use the sentences in the Study box to help you do these exercises.

MEANING

Use <u>four</u> of the words below to complete the meaning of this use of
put somebody or something down:

surface   table   place   holding   keep   floor

to .... somebody or something that you are .... on the
.... or another ....

GRAMMAR

Which of these are grammatically
correct?
a) I put the bag down.
b) I put down the bag.
c) I put it down.
d) I put down it.
e) The bag was put down.

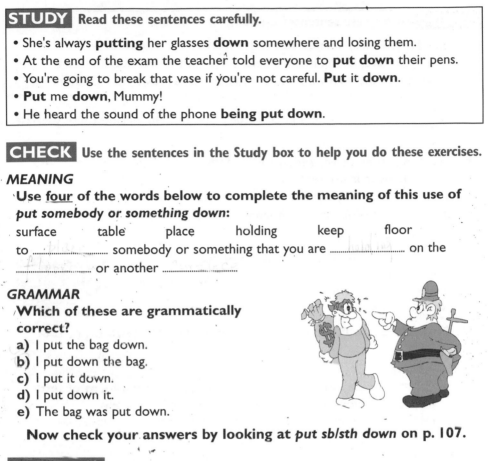

Now check your answers by looking at *put sb/sth down* **on p. 107.**

PRACTISE

Complete these sentences in any way you like, using the verb *put
somebody or something down*:
a) The book was so good that I ....
b) She's got too many things in her hands! Why doesn't she ....?
c) The police told the robbers to ....
d) The baby's gone to sleep on your shoulder. ....

Now check your answers by looking at *put sb/sth down* **on p. 107.**

BUILD YOUR VOCABULARY

OPPOSITES

The opposite of **put somebody or something down** is **pick somebody or
something up**.
*She walked nervously around the room, **picking** things **up** and **putting** them **down**
again.*

SETTLE DOWN

• What Manuela really wanted was to get married and **settle down**.
• I'm going to travel for six months before **settling down** with a career.
• Jack had **settled down** with his new wife in a small town near London.

CHECK Use the sentences in the Study box to help you do these exercises.

MEANING

If a person *settles down*, which of the following might they do? **More than one answer is correct.**

a) get married   **b)** travel a lot   **c)** start living in one place
d) have a lot of boyfriends or girlfriends   **e)** start a family

GRAMMAR

Which of these are grammatically possible?
a) I settled down.
b) I settled myself down.
c) I was settled down.

Now check your answers by looking at *settle down* on p. 108.

PRACTISE

What would you say in the following situations? Use a form of *settle down* in your answers and anything else that is necessary.
a) You want to know when your friend is going to stop living a crazy life.
   When ....*?*
b) You are very surprised that Jim has decided to get married.
   Jim! I never thought ....
c) Your brother is 35, doesn't have a regular job and goes out every night.
   Isn't it time ....*?*
d) You are enjoying life as a college student, especially the parties.
   I don't want ....

Now check your answers by looking at *settle down* on p. 108.

BUILD YOUR VOCABULARY

OTHER MEANINGS

Settle down can also mean 'to become relaxed and confident in a new situation':
Julie's **settled down** *well at her new school.*
It also has the meaning 'to become calmer and less active':
The children finally **settled down** *and started to work quietly.*

SLOW DOWN; SLOW *somebody or something* DOWN

- He realized he was driving too fast and began to **slow down**.
- They claim they can **slow down** the ageing process.
- Can't you work any faster? You're **slowing** the whole class **down**!
- Don't wait for me - I'm only **slowing** you **down**.
- The plant's growth **is slowed down** by lack of light.

CHECK Use the sentences in the Study box to help you do these exercises.

MEANING
What is the opposite of *slow down*?
 a) go quickly   **b)** go more quickly   **c)** go slowly   **d)** go more slowly

GRAMMAR
Which of these are grammatically possible?
 a) He slowed down.
 b) He slowed the car down.
 c) He slowed down the car.
 d) He slowed it down.
 e) He slowed down it.
 f) The car was slowed down.

Now check your answers by looking at *slow down; slow sb/sth down* on p. 108.

PRACTISE

Choose one of the following words to complete each sentence. Only use each word once.

bus   economy   heat   horse   roadworks

 a) The .... slowed down as it approached the crossroads.
 b) The .... in the afternoon always slowed us down.
 c) A recent report shows that the .... has slowed down this year.
 d) The .... are slowing the traffic down in the mornings.
 e) The .... didn't slow down until it had thrown its rider off.

Now check your answers by looking at *slow down; slow sb/sth down* on p. 108.

BUILD YOUR VOCABULARY

RELATED WORDS
noun: **a slowdown** (= a decrease in the rate of activity or production)
This year's figures show a considerable **slowdown**.

SYNONYMS
You can also use the verb **slow up** with the same meaning, but this is less frequent: *The car* **slowed up** *as it drew level with the bank.*

OPPOSITES
The opposite of **slow down** is **speed up**.

TURN *somebody or something* DOWN

STUDY Read these sentences carefully.

- Why did you **turn down** the invitation to Kate and Joe's wedding?
- I can't believe he **turned** the company's offer **down** flat.
- She keeps inviting me to visit her in Scotland but I always **turn** her **down**.
- Their proposals have **been turned down** because they will cost too much.
- I've just **been turned down** for another job.

CHECK Use the sentences in the Study box to help you do these exercises.

MEANING

1 **Choose the correct meaning of this use of** *turn somebody or something down:*

  a) to reject or refuse somebody or something

  b) to remove or destroy somebody or something

2 **Which of the following can you** *turn down?*

  a) an invitation   **b)** an offer   **c)** a party   **d)** a job

  e) a wedding   **f)** a proposal

GRAMMAR

Which of these are grammatically possible?

a) She turned the offer down.

b) She turned down the offer.

c) She turned it down.

d) She turned down him.

e) The offer was turned down.

f) He was turned down.

Now check your answers by looking at *turn sb/sth down* **on p. 109.**

PRACTISE

Complete the following sentences with the correct form of *turn somebody or something down* and one of the objects below:

the band   the plans   the chance   him   a place

a) Every record company had .... so they produced the album themselves.

b) They were very disappointed when the Council .... for a larger school.

c) Early in his career he .... of playing the title role in a Hollywood movie.

d) Sadly, he had to .... on a graduate course when his mother fell ill.

e) She thought he was so attractive that she couldn't imagine any woman ....

Now check your answers by looking at *turn sb/sth down* **on p. 109.**

TURN *something* DOWN

STUDY **Read these sentences carefully.**

- I put the radio on loud, but Dad shouted to me to **turn** the volume **down**.
- He **turned down** the sound on the TV set but left the picture on the screen.
- If the music's too loud for you, why didn't you ask me to **turn** it **down**?
- Victor asked for the lights to **be turned down** low while he sang.

CHECK Use the sentences in the Study box to help you do these exercises.

MEANING

Complete the meaning of this use of *turn something down* by using the words below:

reduce   equipment   noise   controls

to adjust the .... on a piece of .... in order to ....
the amount of heat, ... or light that is produced

GRAMMAR

Which of these are grammatically possible?
a) He turned down.
b) He turned the volume down.
c) He turned down the volume.
d) He turned it down.
e) The volume was turned down.

Now check your answers by looking at *turn sth down* on p. 109.

PRACTISE

Complete the following sentences in an appropriate way, using *turn something down*:
a) I can't hear myself think in here! ....
b) It's very hot in here. Do you mind if .... ?
c) The television was still on, but the sound ,,.. .
d) She didn't want the sauce to boil so she ....
e) He wanted a romantic atmosphere so he put on some music and

....

Now check your answers by looking at *turn sth down* on p. 109.

BUILD YOUR VOCABULARY

OPPOSITES

The opposite of **turn something down** is **turn something up**:
*Every time I **turn** the TV **up** so that I can hear it better, he says it's too loud and **turns** it **down** again.*

15

WRITE *something* DOWN

STUDY Read these sentences carefully.

- Work on your own and **write down** the answers to these questions.
- They told me to **write down** everything the woman had said to me.
- Before I began my story, I **wrote** all my ideas **down**.
- She told him the address and he **wrote** it **down** in his notebook.
- Information was passed on by word of mouth and **was** never **written down**.

CHECK Use the sentences in the Study box to help you do these exercises.

MEANING

Choose one word or phrase from the brackets to complete the meaning of *write something down:*

to write something *(on paper / on a computer)* in order to *(read / remember)* or *(record / reply to)* it

GRAMMAR

Which of these are grammatically possible?
a) He wrote down.
b) He wrote his name down.
c) He wrote down his name.
d) He wrote it down.
e) He wrote down it.
f) His name was written down.

Now check your answers by looking at *write sth down* on p. 110.

PRACTISE

1 Correct any errors in the following:
a) Write new words down is a good way to help you remember them.
b) I'm bound to forget everything if it isn't wrote down.
c) He's always writting things down in that little book. I wonder what?

2 *Write down* or *write*? Look again at the answer to the **MEANING** exercise. The verb *write* is used for the general ability and for creating books and letters. Choose the best verb in these sentences:
a) In some countries children don't start to read or **write/write down** until they are 6.
b) Who **wrote/wrote down** 'Pride and Prejudice'?
c) I can't remember new vocabulary unless I **write it/write it down**.
d) Have you got a piece of paper? I'll **write/write down** my phone number for you.

Now check your answers by looking at *write sth down* on p. 110.

LOOK FOR *somebody or something*

STUDY **Read these sentences carefully.**

- I'm **looking for** my watch. Have you seen it?
- Jack **looked for** his name on the list but couldn't find it.
- Where have you been? We've been **looking for** you everywhere.
- He'd lost some files, and we spent over an hour **looking for** them.
- What are you **looking for**?
- I'm **looking for** a job at the moment, but it's hard to find one that is suitable.

CHECK Use the sentences in the Study box to help you do these exercises.

MEANING
Which of the following means the same as *look for somebody or something*?
a) to watch somebody or something
b) to search for somebody or something
c) to take care of somebody or something

GRAMMAR
Which of these are grammatically possible?
a) He is looking for his brother.
b) He is looking his brother for.
c) He is looking for him.
d) He is looking him for.

Now check your answers by looking at *look for sb/sth* on p. 106.

PRACTISE

1 Complete the following with the correct form of *look for* and one of the phrases below:

her son   her contact lenses   a blue shirt   it   an apartment

a) (In a shop) 'Can I help you?' 'Yes, I ....'
b) Have you seen my black scarf? I've .... everywhere.
c) Clare was on her hands and knees, ...
d) She was frantically ...., who had run off somewhere.
e) My journey to work takes too long. I'm going .... in the centre of town.

2 There is a grammatical mistake in <u>one</u> of these sentences. Can you find the mistake and correct it?
a) If you're looking for a cheap second-hand car, you've come to the right place!
b) Is this the book you were looking for?
c) Sarah lost her keys, so we spent ages looking for it all over the house.

Now check your answers by looking at *look for sb/sth* on p. 106.

LOOK FORWARD TO *something*

STUDY Read these sentences carefully.

- Are you **looking forward to** the wedding?
- I'm **looking forward to** seeing Jane and Peter again, aren't you?
- We're going to France next week. I'm really **looking forward to** it.
- Anna **looked forward to** the day when she could go home.
- I wasn't **looking forward to** going to the dentist again!

CHECK Use the sentences in the Study box to help you do these exercises.

MEANING

Choose the best explanation of the meaning of *look forward to something*:

a) to look at something that is in front of you
b) to feel excited about something that is going to happen in the future
c) to think about something that might happen in the future

GRAMMAR

Which of these are grammatically possible?

a) She's looking forward to the party.
b) She's looking forward to it.
c) She's looking forward to leave.
d) She's looking forward to leaving.

Now check your answers by looking at *look forward to sth* **on p. 106.**

PRACTISE

1 **Only <u>one</u> of the following sentences is correct. Which one? Can you find and correct the errors in the other sentences?**

a) I'm looking forward the party very much - all my friends are coming.
b) What time is your brother arriving? I'm really looking forward to meet him.
c) Finally the day of the wedding arrived. I'd been looking forward to it for ages.
d) The mail only came once a week, so we always looked forward to.

2 **Is there anything <u>you</u> are looking forward to? What are you <u>not</u> looking forward to? Write some sentences about yourself, using this verb.**

....

....

Now check your answers by looking at *look forward to sth* **on p. 106.**

BUILD YOUR VOCABULARY

OTHER MEANINGS

Look forward to is used very often at the end of formal letters:

I **look forward to** *hearing from you soon.*
Looking forward to *meeting you next week.*

CHECK IN; CHECK *somebody or something* IN

STUDY Read these sentences carefully.

- It's a good idea to **check in** two hours before your flight is due to leave.
- The telephone kept ringing as he was trying to **check** the guests **in**.
- I watched the car leave, then went to **check in** my suitcases.
- Has she **checked** you **in** yet?
- All the passengers have **been checked in** now.

CHECK Use the sentences in the Study box to help you do these exercises.

MEANING

Check in means 'to go to an official desk at a hotel or an airport and tell somebody that you have arrived'.

1 If you *check somebody in*, what do you do? Choose the best meaning.
  a) you make sure they are in the correct place, are doing things correctly, etc.
  b) you take sb's name, check their reservation, give them a key, documents, etc.

2 If you *check something in*, what do you do? Choose the best meaning.
  a) you leave or accept luggage to be put on a plane
  b) you deliver something to someone

GRAMMAR

Which of these are grammatically possible?
  a) I checked in
  b) I checked my bags in.
  c) I checked in my bags.
  d) I checked them in.
  e) I checked in them.
  f) The bags were checked in.

Now check your answers by looking at *check in; check sb/sth in* on p. 101.

PRACTISE

In <u>two</u> of these sentences the verb *check in* is not used correctly. Can you find the mistakes and correct them?
  a) We checked in Heathrow at 2 p.m. but our plane didn't leave until nine.
  b) You must never agree to check in other people's baggage.
  c) Let's check our bags in first, then have a look at the shops.
  d) After checking us in and having a quick shower, we went off to explore.

Now check your answers by looking at *check in; check sb/sth in* on p. 101.

BUILD YOUR VOCABULARY

RELATED WORDS
noun: **check-in** *(This noun can be countable or uncountable.)*
Check-in *is from 11.30.*

OPPOSITES
➤ **check out, check out of something**

FILL *something* IN

STUDY Read these sentences carefully.

- You have to **fill in** a registration form before you can use the library.
- **Fill in** the blanks with the correct word or phrase.
- Please **fill in** your personal details for our records.
- That tax form is very complicated. Do you need any help **filling** it **in**?
- I had to send the form back, as it hadn't **been filled in** correctly.

CHECK Use the sentences in the Study box to help you do these exercises.

MEANING
Use the words below to complete the meaning of this use of *fill something in*:

writing   complete   form   information

to .... a document (for example a .... or a questionnaire)

by writing the necessary .... on it

GRAMMAR
Which of these are grammatically possible?
a) He filled in the form.
'ɔ) He filled it in.
c) He filled in it.
d) The form was filled in.

Now check your answers by looking at *fill sth in* on p. 103.

PRACTISE

Complete the following with the correct form of *fill something in* and one of the objects below:

her name   your personal details   it   their forms   our questionnaire

a) Once you have ...., click 'OK' to continue.

b) Here is the entry form, and here are some notes to help you

....

c) Thank you for .... This will help us to improve our services.

d) He .... on the invitation and put it in an envelope.

e) About 35% of people had .... incorrectly.

Now check your answers by looking at *fill sth in* on p. 103.

BUILD YOUR VOCABULARY

SYNONYMS
You can use **fill out a form** instead of **fill in a form**:
*We've got lots of forms to **fill out**.*
*Simply **fill out** this questionnaire and return it to us by post.*

GET IN; GET IN *something*

STUDY Read these sentences carefully.

- How did the burglars **get in**? Did they break a window?
- He **got in** the truck and drove off.
- It's not a very big car. Do you think all five of us will **get in** it?

CHECK Use the sentences in the Study box to help you do these exercises.

MEANING

1 *Get in* usually means 'to enter or go inside'. Which of the following can you get *in*?

a) a car   **b)** a bicycle   **c)** a building   **d)** a room   **e)** a sofa
f) a chair

2 Which of the following is closest in meaning to the sentence '*They got in the building*'?

a) They had to enter the building.
b) They tried to enter the building.
c) They managed to enter the building.

GRAMMAR

Which of these are grammatically possible?

a) We got in.
b) We got in the car.
c) We got it in.
d) We got in it.
e) The car was got in.

Now check your answers by looking at *get in; get in sth* on p. 103.

PRACTISE

Complete these sentences with the correct form of *get in* and an object (a noun or a pronoun) if necessary:

a) Quick! .... and fasten your seatbelt!
b) She .... and asked the driver to take her to the station.
c) If you want to go to the museum, you can .... free on Sundays.
d) Oh no! Hide! I'll go under the bed and you ....!

Now check your answers by looking at *get in; get in sth* on p. 103.

BUILD YOUR VOCABULARY

OPPOSITES
➤ *get out; get out of something*

SIMILAR VERBS
Also look at the verb **get on; get on something**, which has a similar meaning.

CUT *somebody* OFF

STUDY **Read these sentences carefully.**

- The day I had to work on the switchboard I kept **cutting** people **off**!
- Kenneth slammed the phone down and **cut** her **off**.
- Operator, I've just **been cut off**. Can you reconnect me?

CHECK **Use the sentences in the Study box to help you do these exercises.**

MEANING

Complete the explanation of this meaning of *cut somebody off* by choosing two words from the list below:

interrupt   continue   making   breaking

to .... a telephone conversation by ....

the connection

GRAMMAR

Which of these are grammatically possible?
a) She cut her friend off.
b) She cut off her friend.
c) She cut him off.
d) She cut off him.
e) She was cut off.

Now check your answers by looking at *cut sb off* on p. 102.

PRACTISE

Rewrite the following sentences so that the meaning stays the same, using a form of *cut somebody off*:
a) Their telephone connection was suddenly broken.
   They ....
b) Operator, the connection with the person I was talking to has been broken.
   Operator, we ....
c) I'm so sorry. My son was playing with the phone and broke our connection.
   I'm so sorry. My son ....

Now check your answers by looking at *cut sb off* on p. 102.

BUILD YOUR VOCABULARY

OTHER MEANINGS

Cut somebody off can also mean 'to interrupt somebody when they are speaking':

*He rudely **cut** me **off** in mid-sentence.*
*He put his hand over her mouth to **cut off** her cry of fear.*
*My explanation for why I was late **was** abruptly **cut off**.*

CUT *somebody or something* OFF

FIRST MEANING

STUDY Read these sentences carefully.

- A concrete wall **cut** the town **off** from the beach and the sea.
- No one knew why Ray had **cut off** all contact with his family.
- The mist had **cut** them **off** from the rest of the group, and they were lost.
- Pierre **cut** himself **off** by living in Scotland, far away from his family.
- The farm **is** often completely **cut off** in the winter.

CHECK Use the sentences in the Study box to help you do these exercises.

MEANING
Complete this meaning of *cut somebody or something off* by putting the words below into the correct place:

physically   things   separate   people

to .... somebody, something or yourself ....
or socially from other .... or ....

GRAMMAR
Which of these are grammatically possible?
a) Snow cut the town off.
b) Snow cut off the town.
c) Snow cut it off.
d) Snow cut off it.
e) He cut himself off.
f) He cut off himself.
g) The town was cut off.

Now check your answers by looking at *cut sb/sth off* on p. 102.

PRACTISE

1 Which of the answers below would be logical in reply to the following question? More than one answer is possible.

> *Why has he cut himself off from his friends and family?*

a) He wanted to be alone.
b) He loved them very much.
c) He was angry with them.
d) He needed them.

2 Only <u>one</u> of these sentences is grammatically correct. Which one? Can you find and correct the mistakes in the other sentences?
a) We are often cutting off in the winter because of bad weather.
b) You can't expect me to cut completely myself off from my friends.
c) They were so busy talking to each other that I felt cut off and alone.
d) The country had cut off from all contact with the outside world.

Now check your answers by looking at *cut sb/sth off* on p. 102.

CUT *somebody or something* OFF

SECOND MEANING

STUDY **Read these sentences carefully.**

- They **cut off** the water supply for three hours this morning.
- The gas company won't **cut** you **off** without warning you first.
- He had forgotten to pay the bill so his phone had **been cut off**.
- I was told that our research funds were **being cut off** immediately.

CHECK Use the sentences in the Study box to help you do these exercises.

MEANING

1 **Choose the best meaning for this use of *cut somebody or something off*:**
  a) to stop having something
  b) to stop making something for somebody
  c) to stop the supply of something to somebody

2 **Which of the following can be *cut off*?**
  a) electricity   b) water   c) lights   d) gas   e) telephone
  f) television   g) funds

GRAMMAR
Which of these are grammatically possible?
  a) They cut off the electricity supply.
  b) They cut us off.
  c) They cut off us.
  d) The electricity supply was cut off.

Now check your answers by looking at *cut sb/sth off* on p. 102.

PRACTISE

1 **Answer the following questions, using an appropriate form of *cut off* and any other necessary information:**
  a) Why are you going out to use a public telephone?
     Because ....
  b) What happens if you don't pay your electricity bill?
     The company ....
  c) Why can't we cook dinner at home?
     Because the gas ....

2 **Correct any errors in the following:**
  a) The power is automatically cut off if the system overheats.
  b) She didn't pay the bill so they cut off.
  c) Water supplies to farmers were cut off last week to try to conserve water.
  d) They were wearing coats and scarves as the electricity was been cut off.

Now check your answers by looking at *cut sb/sth off* on p. 102.

DROP *somebody or something* OFF

STUDY Read these sentences carefully.

- Will you **drop** the kids **off** at school on your way into town?
- We **dropped off** our bags at the hotel and then went to explore the city.
- You can **drop** me **off** here if you like. It's not far to walk.
- Where would you like to **be dropped off**?

CHECK Use the sentences in the Study box to help you do these exercises.

MEANING

1 If you *drop somebody off,* what do you do? Choose the best meaning.
  a) you take somebody in your car and leave them somewhere
  b) you make or help somebody leave a place

2 If you *drop something off,* what do you do? Choose the best meaning.
  a) you let something fall out of your hand
  b) you deliver something somewhere

GRAMMAR

Which of these are grammatically possible?
  a) I dropped my friends off.
  b) I dropped off my friends.
  c) I dropped them off.
  d) I dropped off them.
  e) They were dropped off.

Now check your answers by looking at *drop sb/sth off* on p. 103.

PRACTISE

1 **Complete these sentences using an appropriate form of *drop off* and a suitable object (a noun or a pronoun):**
  a) Could you .... outside the hotel, please?
  b) I work near the library. Shall I .... for you?
  c) 'Where ....?' 'Just here will be fine, thanks.'

2 **There is a grammatical mistake in <u>one</u> of these sentences. Can you find the mistake and correct it?**
  a) I was dropped off right outside my house, which was great.
  b) Oh no! I forgot to drop off that package for my boss!
  c) Sue's driving - why don't you ask her to drop off?

Now check your answers by looking at *drop sb/sth off* on p. 103.

BUILD YOUR VOCABULARY

OPPOSITES

The opposite of **drop somebody or something off** is **pick somebody or something up**:
*Parents can **drop off** or **pick up** their children outside the school.*

GET OFF; GET OFF *something*

| STUDY | Read these sentences carefully. |

- Is this where we **get off**?
- Your bike's got a flat tyre. You'd better **get off** and walk.
- The teenager was last seen **getting off** a train in Liverpool.
- The bus stopped and three people **got off** it.

CHECK Use the sentences in the Study box to help you do these exercises.

MEANING

1 Which one of the following means the same as *to get off a train*?

  a) to leave a train   **b)** to board a train   **c)** to travel on a train

2 Which of the following can you *get off*?

  a) a horse   **b)** a train   **c)** a car   **d)** a plane   **e)** a bicycle   **f)** a ship

  g) a truck   **h)** a tram

GRAMMAR

Which of these are grammatically possible?

a) He got off.

b) He got the train off.

c) He got off the train.

d) He got it off.

e) He got off it.

f) The train was got off.

  Now check your answers by looking at *get off; get off sth* on p. 103.

PRACTISE

  Complete these sentences with the correct form of *get off* and an object (a noun or a pronoun) where necessary:

  a) There was a problem at the airport when we landed, and they wouldn't let us

  ....

  b) You can ask the driver where ....

  c) Sorry I'm late. I .... at the wrong stop, and had to walk.

  d) You can't cycle here! .... at once!

  Now check your answers by looking at *get off; get off sth* on p. 103.

BUILD YOUR VOCABULARY

OPPOSITES

➤ **get on, get on something**

SIMILAR VERBS

Also look at the verb **get out; get out of something**, which has a similar meaning.

26

GO OFF

FIRST MEANING

STUDY **STUDY** Read these sentences carefully.

- The gun **went off** accidentally while he was holding it.
- I heard that a bomb had **gone off** in the centre of town.
- 'What's that noise?' 'I think it's fireworks **going off** in the park.'
- My alarm clock **goes off** every morning at seven.
- Everybody had to leave the building when the fire alarm **went off**.

CHECK Use the sentences in the Study box to help you do these exercises.

MEANING

1 Complete the meanings with a word or phrase from the brackets:

a) If a bomb goes off, it .... *(falls / explodes)*

b) If a gun goes off, it is .... *(dropped / fired)*

c) If an alarm goes off, it makes a sudden .... *(loud noise / explosion)*

2 Which of the following can go off?

a) a fire   b) a bomb   c) a gun   d) a loud noise

e) fireworks   f) a radio

GRAMMAR

Which of these are grammatically possible?

a) The bomb went off.

b) He went off the bomb.

c) The bomb was gone off.

Now check your answers by looking at *go off* on p. 104.

PRACTISE

Complete these sentences in an appropriate way, using the verb *go off* and any other necessary information:

a) I just heard a loud bang. It sounded as if ....

b) Be careful with those fireworks! They might ....

c) Sorry I'm late. My alarm ....

d) The thieves ran away when ....

Now check your answers by looking at *go off* on p. 104.

BUILD YOUR VOCABULARY

OTHER MEANINGS

Go off can also be used with a similar meaning to describe something making a sudden flash:

*When he finished his song, flashbulbs **went off** in the audience* (= from cameras).

GO OFF

STUDY **Read these sentences carefully.**

- Put the food in the fridge, otherwise it will **go off**.
- Can you smell this milk? I think it might have **gone off**.
- How are we going to stop the meat **going off** in this heat?

CHECK **Use the sentences in the Study box to help you do these exercises.**

MEANING

1 **If food or drink** *goes off*, **which of the following are true? More than one answer is correct.**
   a) it tastes bad
   b) it smells bad
   c) someone has eaten it
   d) it is not fit to eat or drink
   e) it is in the wrong place

2 **Which of the following can** *go off*?
   a) fish   **b)** eggs   **c)** a cow   **d)** beef   **e)** toast   **f)** cream

GRAMMAR
   Which of these are grammatically possible?
   a) Milk goes off quickly.
   b) Milk goes off freshness quickly.
   c) The milk was gone off.

   Now check your answers by looking at *go off* **on p. 104.**

PRACTISE

   Complete this conversation in an appropriate way, using a form of *go off* **in each response and any other necessary information:**
   a) Let's have chicken for dinner.
      We can't, the chicken ....
   b) Well, perhaps we can cook the salmon?
      I'm afraid ....
   c) How about an omelette? Are the eggs fresh?
      No, ...
   d) Let's just have a cup of tea then.
      We can't, ...

   Now check your answers by looking at *go off* **on p. 104.**

BUILD YOUR VOCABULARY

SIMILAR VERBS
You can also use **be off** to describe food that is not fit to eat:
*This tea tastes funny. I think the milk **is off**.*

LOG OFF; LOG OFF *something*

STUDY Read these sentences carefully.

- Don't forget to **log off** when you've finished using the computer.
- How do I **log off** from the databank?
- **Logging off** the website will return you to the first page.
- If you don't like this site, just **log off** it.

CHECK Use the sentences in the Study box to help you do these exercises.

MEANING

Choose the best word to complete the meaning of *log off*:

start   finish   end   continue

to perform the actions that allow you to .... using a computer system

GRAMMAR

Which of these are grammatically possible?

a) I logged off.
b) I logged the computer off.
c) I logged off the computer.
d) I logged it off
e) I logged off it.

This verb is also common in the pattern **be logged off**: *You are now **logged off**.*

Now check your answers by looking at *log off; log off sth* on p. 106.

PRACTISE

Complete these sentences with the correct form of *log off*. Use the objects below <u>where necessary</u>:

our website   the Internet

a) Teenagers are .... in millions because they can't buy things as they had hoped.
b) You might have to wait until one of the other users ....
c) You have just .... and ended your session. Come back soon!

Now check your answers by looking at *log off; log off sth* on p 106.

BUILD YOUR VOCABULARY

SYNONYMS

Log out; log out of something has the same meaning and is used in the same variety of patterns:
*You have successfully **logged out of** the system.*
*You **are** already **logged out**.*

OPPOSITES

The opposite of **log off** is **log on**:
*If your system is running slowly, try **logging off** and then **logging on** again.*

PUT *somebody* **OFF;** **PUT** *somebody* **OFF** *something*

FIRST MEANING

> ### STUDY Read these sentences carefully.
>
> - His manner tends to **put** people **off**.
> - Don't tell Lisa how hard the course is - you'll **put** her **off**!
> - They did their best to **put** their son **off** the idea of acting as a career.
> - It's the smell of garlic that **puts** most people **off** it.
> - The accident **put** me **off** driving for a long time.
> - Don't **be put off** by his appearance - he's really very nice.

CHECK Use the sentences in the Study box to help you do these exercises.

MEANING
Use the words below to complete this meaning of *put somebody off*:

interested   liking   stop

to make somebody .... or being .... in
somebody or something

GRAMMAR
Which of these are grammatically possible?
a) It put John off.
b) It put John off his food.
c) It put John off to eat his food.
d) It put John off eating his food.
e) It put him off.
f) John was put off.

Now check your answers by looking at *put sb off; put sb off sth* **on p. 107.**

PRACTISE

Complete each sentence using *put somebody off* **and anything else necessary, so that the meaning stays the same:**
a) After the accident James didn't want to ride a bike for a long time.
   The accident ....
b) Don't worry about the cost of the book.
   Don't be ....
c) I stopped liking him because of his political views.
   His political views ....

Now check your answers by looking at *put sb off; put sb off sth* **on p. 107.**

BUILD YOUR VOCABULARY

RELATED WORDS
adjective: **off-putting**
He seemed friendly enough, but he had a rather **off-putting** *manner.*

30

PUT *somebody* OFF; PUT *somebody* OFF *something*

SECOND MEANING

STUDY Read these sentences carefully.

- The manager complained that the noise of the crowd had **put** his players **off**.
- Don't stand there watching me - you're **putting** me **off**!
- The loud music **put** Ben **off** his work.
- In the exam I **was** rather **put off** by somebody coughing.

CHECK Use the sentences in the Study box to help you do these exercises.

MEANING

Choose the correct meaning for this use of *put somebody off*:

a) to disturb somebody who is trying to give all their attention to something

b) to cancel something that you have arranged with somebody

GRAMMAR

Which of these are grammatically possible?

a) The noise put Ben off.

b) The noise put off Ben.

c) The noise put Ben off his work.

d) The noise put him off.

e) Ben was put off.

Now check your answers by looking at *put sb off; put sb off sth* on p. 107.

PRACTISE

1 Complete the following sentences in an appropriate way, using a form of *put somebody off* and any other necessary words or phrases:

a) How can you work while the TV's on? Doesn't ....?

b) I don't want my friends to come and watch me play. They ....

c) I didn't realize you were trying to work. I can turn the radio off
if ....

2 Correct any errors in the following:

a) If I want to do well, I mustn't let anything put off my work this week.

b) It had started to rain, but this didn't put her off her game at all.

c) The children all sat at the front and tried to put off the teacher.

d) The noise of the traffic is putting her off, so she closed the window.

Now check your answers by looking at *put sb off; put sb off sth* on p. 107.

BUILD YOUR VOCABULARY

RELATED WORDS

adjective: **off-putting**

Some children find it **off-putting** *to have a teacher watching them while they work.*

PUT *something* OFF

STUDY Read these sentences carefully.

- It's very easy to **put** difficult decisions **off**.
- They've decided to **put off** their wedding until March.
- You'll have to go to the dentist eventually. Why keep **putting** it **off**?
- Some couples **put off** having children until they are older.
- They were going to start building, but the work has **been put off** again.

CHECK Use the sentences in the Study box to help you do these exercises.

MEANING
Which of these verbs means the same as *put something off*?
a) to cancel something **b)** to delay something **c)** to refuse something
d) to prevent something

GRAMMAR
Which of these are grammatically possible?
a) She put her visit off.
b) She put off her visit.
c) She put it off.
d) She put off it.
e) Her visit was put off.

Now check your answers by looking at *put sth off* on p. 107.

PRACTISE

1 **Rewrite the parts of the sentences in italics so that the meaning stays the same, using a form of *put something off* and an object (a noun or a pronoun):**
   a) I'm afraid I have no time for the meeting today. *Can we leave it until tomorrow?*

   ....

   b) This job must be done today - *it cannot be delayed any longer*.

   ....

   c) *I always wait until the last minute to do my work*.

   ....

2 **What do you *put off*? Look at the two examples and write three more sentences that are true for you.**
   a) I hate cleaning the bathroom so I always put it off.
   b) I never put off paying my bills.
   c) ....
   d) ....
   e) ....
   Now check your answers by looking at *put sth off* on p. 107.

SET OFF

* When are you planning to **set off**?
* I usually **set off** for college at about seven.
* They quickly got in the car and **set off** down the road.
* We unpacked and changed our clothes before **setting off** to explore.

CHECK Use the sentences in the Study box to help you do these exercises.

MEANING

Choose <u>two</u> of the words below to complete the meaning of this use of *set off*:

journey   begin   holiday   end   job   arrange

to .... a ....

GRAMMAR

Which of these are grammatically possible?

a) He set off.
b) He set off the journey.
c) The journey set off.

Now check your answers by looking at *set off* on p. 108.

PRACTISE

1 **Complete these sentences with a form of *set off* and one of the prepositions below. Use each preposition <u>once</u> only.**

at   on   up   for   until

a) After breakfast they .... the mountain.
b) Do you want something to eat before you .... work?
c) He finally .... the first stage of his round-the-world trip.
d) Every morning she .... 6 a.m. in order to miss the rush-hour traffic.
e) I'm not surprised we're late. We didn't .... 8 o'clock!

2 **Answer the following questions about yourself, using the verb *set off***

a) What time do you leave for school/college/work every day?

....

b) You are going shopping with a friend. What time will you leave home?

....

Now check your answers by looking at *set off* on p. 108.

BUILD YOUR VOCABULARY

SYNONYMS

Set out means the same as **set off**, but is more often used about a long journey:
*He **set out** on the last stage of his round-the-world trip.*

TAKE OFF

STUDY Read these sentences carefully.

- What time is your flight due to **take off**?
- We were a bit late **taking off**.
- The plane eventually **took off** at 5 p.m.

CHECK Use the sentences in the Study box to help you do these exercises.

MEANING

1 Use <u>two</u> of the words below to complete this meaning of *take off*:

touch   fly   leave   move

to .... the ground and begin to ....

2 According to the meaning above, which of the following can *take off* in this way?

a) an aircraft   **b)** a ball   **c)** a bird   **d)** a train   **e)** a bomb

GRAMMAR

Which of these are grammatically possible?

a) The plane took off.

b) We took off.

c) We took off the plane.

d) The plane took off the ground.

Now check your answers by looking at *take off* on p. 109.

PRACTISE

1 Match the two halves to make complete sentences:

a) In the end we	**i)** take off at all.
b) It was 10 p.m.	**ii)** took off on time.
c) Apparently the flight didn't	**iii)** taking off.
d) We were a bit late	**iv)** when we finally took off.

2 Explain to your friend why you were late arriving in Paris:

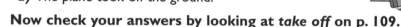

....

Now check your answers by looking at *take off* on p. 109.

BUILD YOUR VOCABULARY

RELATED WORDS

noun: **take-off** *(This noun can be countable or uncountable.)*
*I hate flying, but fortunately it was a nice smooth **take-off**.*
*We are now ready for **take-off**.*

OPPOSITES

The opposite of **take off** is **land**:
*It was raining when we **took off** in Paris, but sunny when we **landed** in London.*

TAKE *something* **OFF**

STUDY **Read these sentences carefully.**

- Why don't you **take** your coat **off**?
- Do you mind if I **take off** my shoes?
- She loved her new scarf so much that she refused to **take** it **off** at bedtime.
- All jewellery must **be taken off** when doing sports.

CHECK **Use the sentences in the Study box to help you do these exercises.**

MEANING

1 Which of these verbs is closest in meaning to *take off*?

a) to remove   **b)** to collect   **c)** to wear   **d)** to leave

2 Which of the following can you <u>not</u> take off?

a) gloves   **b)** necklace   **c)** sunglasses   **d)** contact lenses

GRAMMAR

Which of these are grammatically possible?
a) He took his tie off.
b) He took off his tie.
c) He took it off.
d) He took off it.
e) His tie was taken off.

    Now check your answers by looking at *take sth off* **on p. 109.**

PRACTISE

Respond to the following, using *take something off* and the information in brackets in an appropriate way in each case. Add any other words you think you need. The first one has been done for you.
a) Do you need some help?
    Yes, please. I.. (my boots).
    Yes, please. I'm trying to take my boots off.
b) It's so hot in here!
    Why .... (your sweater)?
c) Why aren't you wearing your ring?
    I always..(wash my hands).
d) Is the office warm enough for you?
    No. That's why I .... (my coat).

    Now check your answers by looking at *take sth off* **on p. 109.**

BUILD YOUR VOCABULARY

OPPOSITES

The opposite of **take something off** is **put something on**:
*Aya stopped at the door, **took off** her shoes and **put on** her slippers.*

TELL *somebody* OFF

- If anyone **tells** Sonia **off**, she goes and hides in her room.
- The manager **tells** you **off** if you arrive late.
- Dad often **told** us **off** about watching too much TV.
- Jack's always **getting told off** at school for talking in class.

CHECK Use the sentences in the Study box to help you do these exercises.

MEANING

Choose the best meaning of *tell somebody off*:

a) to speak angrily to somebody because they have done something wrong
b) to ask somebody to go away because you are angry with them

GRAMMAR

Which of these are grammatically possible?
a) She told Jane off.
b) She told off Jane.
c) She told him off.
d) She told off him.
e) Jane was told off.

Now check your answers by looking at *tell sb off* on p. 109.

PRACTISE

1 Complete the following sentences with an appropriate form of *tell somebody off* and one of the objects below:

everyone   me   you   the children

a) If she sees you leaving early, she ....
b) Why are you always ....? I don't deserve it!
c) She .... because they didn't put their toys away.
d) The teacher suddenly got really angry and ....!

2 What do/did your parents or teachers tell <u>you</u> off for? Look at the examples below, and write some similar sentences about yourself, using *tell somebody off* in an appropriate form:

a) My mother tells me off *for not tidying my room*.
b) The teacher told us off *if we didn't do our homework*.

....

....

Now check your answers by looking at *tell sb off* on p. 109.

BUILD YOUR VOCABULARY

RELATED WORDS

noun: **a telling-off**
*Be careful! You've already had one **telling-off** from Dad today, you don't want another!*

TURN *something* OFF

STUDY Read these sentences carefully.

- Can you **turn** the lights **off**? The switch is by the door.
- Somebody forgot to **turn off** the tap in the bathroom.
- You've been watching TV all day! **Turn** it **off** now.
- The TV was on, but the sound had **been turned off**.

CHECK Use the sentences in the Study box to help you do these exercises.

MEANING
Complete this meaning of *turn something off* using the words below:

electricity   button   stop   switch

to .... the flow of ...., gas or water by moving a ....
or pressing a ....

GRAMMAR
Which of these are grammatically possible?
a) He turned the TV off.
b) He turned off the TV.
c) He turned it off.
d) He turned off It.
e) The TV was turned off.

Now check your answers by looking at *turn sth off* on p. 109.

PRACTISE

1 Respond to the following comments by completing the sentences below, using *turn off* and a suitable object (a noun or a pronoun) in each answer:
a) This TV programme is terrible!
    I agree. Let's ....
b) Have you finished with the computer?
    No, don't ....
c) The water is still running!
    Sorry. I forgot ....

2 How many of these comments can you follow with 'Turn it off.'?
a) It's the middle of summer and the heating's on!
b) I've seen this programme before.
c) I can't hear what the newsreader is saying.

Now check your answers by looking at *turn sth off* on p. 109.

BUILD YOUR VOCABULARY

OPPOSITES
➤ **turn something on**

SIMILAR VERBS
➤ **turn something down** and **turn something up**

COME ON

STUDY Read these sentences carefully.

- **Come on!** We'll be late if we don't hurry up!
- **Come on,** Andy, give us a smile. Everything's going to be OK.
- '**Come on**', urged Laura, 'Don't be shy!'
- Oh **come on!** You don't expect me to believe that story, do you?
- You thought the movie was good? Oh **come on**, it was terrible!

CHECK Use the sentences in the Study box to help you do these exercises.

MEANING

The phrase *come on* is used for different reasons. Which <u>one</u> of the following is it <u>not</u> used for?
a) to encourage somebody to do something
b) to show that you are thinking about something
c) to show that you do not believe what somebody has said
d) to show that you disagree with somebody

GRAMMAR

Which of these are grammatically possible?
a) Come on.
b) Oh coming on!
c) They came on.
d) They were come on.

Now check your answers by looking at *come on* on p. 102.

PRACTISE

1 In which of these situations might you tell somebody to *come on*?
a) when you are having a discussion or an argument
b) when you are in a hurry
c) when you are trying to be very polite

2 Is *come on* appropriate in these situations? Choose the best phrase for each.
a) *Come on! / Slow down!* Why are you taking so long?
b) *Oh come on! / Absolutely!* I completely agree.
c) Let's have a drink! *Come on! / Don't have one!*
d) *Come on! / Keep quiet!* Tell me what happened!
e) What are you doing up there? *Come on! / Come down!*

Now check your answers by looking at *come on* on p. 102.

BUILD YOUR VOCABULARY

SYNONYMS

You can also use the verb **come along**, especially in British English:
Come on/along now, don't be afraid.
Come on/along children, you'll be late for school.

GET ON

Read these sentences carefully.

- Do you **get on** with all the people you work with?
- Sarah and I **got on** well, and I missed her when she left.
- She's not **getting on** very well with her parents at the moment.
- How are you and Peter **getting on**?
- The three children **get on** very well together.

CHECK Use the sentences in the Study box to help you do these exercises.

MEANING

Use <u>one</u> of the words below to complete this meaning of *get on*:

bad   friendly   family   difficult

to have a .... relationship with somebody

GRAMMAR

Which of these are grammatically possible?

a) They get on.
b) They get on well.
c) They get on their colleagues.
d) They get on with their colleagues.
e) Their colleagues are got on well with.

Now check your answers by looking at *get on* **on p. 103.**

PRACTISE

1 Match the two halves to make complete sentences:

a) My next-door neighbour and I   **i)** but we're very different.
b) My brother and I get on quite well   **ii)** with my mother than my father.
c) I've always got on very well   **iii)** with my sister-in-law.
d) I used to get on better   **iv)** don't get on at all.

2 Who do you get on with? Who don't you get on very well with? Write some sentences about <u>yourself</u>, using this verb. Use the complete sentences from the last exercise as examples to follow.

....

....

....

Now check your answers by looking at *get on* **on p. 103.**

BUILD YOUR VOCABULARY

SYNONYMS

You can use the particle **along** instead of **on**, especially in American English:
*Russ and I have always **got along** really well.*

GET ON; GET ON *something*

STUDY Read these sentences carefully.

- The bus stopped to let more people **get on**.
- A young woman **got on** at the next station, but there were no seats left.
- Her mobile phone rang just as she was **getting on** the train.
- He **got on** his motorbike and rode away.
- The bus was so full that we couldn't even **get on** it.

CHECK Use the sentences in the Study box to help you do these exercises.

MEANING

1 **Which of the following means the same as *to get on a train*?**

   a) to leave a train   **b)** to board a train   **c)** to travel on a train

2 **Which of these can you *get on*?**

   a) a horse   **b)** a train   **c)** a car   **d)** a plane   **e)** a bicycle   **f)** a ship
   g) a truck   **h)** a tram

GRAMMAR

Which of these are grammatically possible?
a) We got on.
b) We got on the bus.
c) We got it on.
d) We got on it.
e) The bus was got on.

Now check your answers by looking at *get on; get on sth* on p. 103.

PRACTISE

Complete these sentences with the correct form of *get on* and an object (a noun or a pronoun) if necessary:
a) He .... and cycled off down the road.
b) We waited in the departure lounge for two hours before they let us
....
c) This train leaves in two minutes, so we'd better ....
d) I .... that took me straight to the airport from the main bus station.
e) I think this bus goes to the city centre. Shall we ....?

Now check your answers by looking at *get on; get on sth* on p. 103.

BUILD YOUR VOCABULARY

OPPOSITES
➤ *get off; get off something*

SIMILAR VERBS
Also look at the verb **get in, get in something**, which has a similar meaning.

40

GO ON

FIRST MEANING

Read these sentences carefully.

- I know things seem bad, but life must **go on**.
- Things can't **go on** as they are. Something has to change.
- He didn't even look up. He just **went on** reading.
- She just **went on** with what she was doing as if I wasn't there.

CHECK Use the sentences in the Study box to help you do these exercises.

MEANING
Match each sentence below with the appropriate meaning of the verb
go on:
a) The situation went on for many years.   i) to continue without stopping
b) She went on painting.   ii) to continue to happen or exist

GRAMMAR
Which of these are grammatically possible?
a) He went on.
b) The work went on.
c) He went on working.
d) He went on with his work.
e) He went on to work.

Now check your answers by looking at *go on* on p. 104.

PRACTISE

1 Match the two halves to make mini dialogues:
a) You can't go on lying to him.   i) How rude!
b) She went on talking.   ii) Yes, it's time to tell him the truth.
c) We can't go on like this!   iii) Why? What's wrong?

2 Complete the following in an appropriate way, using the verb *go on*:
a) It's time for some changes around here. Things ....
b) When I walked into the room, everybody ....

Now check your answers by looking at *go on* on p. 104.

BUILD YOUR VOCABULARY

RELATED WORDS
adjective: **ongoing** (= continuing to exist or develop)
*Modernizing the computer system is an **ongoing** process.*

SYNONYMS
Carry on has the same meaning and is used in the same way:
*He **carried on** talking, even though I asked him to stop.*

OTHER MEANINGS
Go on can also mean 'to last': *The class **goes on** until nine o'clock.*

41

GO ON

SECOND MEANING

Read these sentences carefully.

- What's **going on** here?
- He never told me what **went on** at school.
- Something was **going on** and I wanted to know what.
- The public have a right to know what **goes on** behind the scenes.

CHECK Use the sentences in the Study box to help you do these exercises.

MEANING
Which one of these verbs means the same as *go on*?

a) to appear   **b)** to happen   **c)** to exist

GRAMMAR
Which of these are grammatically possible?

a) Something is going on.
b) Somebody is going on.
c) Nothing is going on.
d) Something was gone on.

Now check your answers by looking at *go on* on p. 105.

PRACTISE

1 Match the two halves to make complete sentences:

a) The public meeting gave us a chance	**i)** what went on while I was away.
b) She's been very quiet lately. Do you think	**ii)** what's going on?
c) Everybody came running to see	**iii)** to find out what was going on.
d) Don't you think people should know	**iv)** what was going on.
e) I have no idea	**v)** there's something going on?

2 Complete these sentences in an appropriate way, using *go on* in each:

a) I can hear somebody screaming. ....?
b) Why is she so suspicious? There ....
c) It was a long time ago, and I never discovered ....

Now check your answers by looking at *go on* on p. 105.

BUILD YOUR VOCABULARY

RELATED WORDS
noun: **goings-on** (= activities or events that are strange or amusing) *(This is a plural noun.)*
*There have been some strange **goings-on** at their house.*

HAVE *something* ON; HAVE GOT *something* ON

STUDY Read these sentences carefully.

- She didn't **have** any lipstick **on**, which was unusual.
- I **had on** a pair of jeans and a T-shirt.
- You've seen my black dress. I **had it on** yesterday.
- I can't see that. I **haven't got** my glasses **on**.

CHECK Use the sentences in the Study box to help you do these exercises.

MEANING

I Which of these sentences means the same as '*She had a new hat on.*'?
  a) She was wearing a new hat.
  b) She had a new hat.
  c) She bought a new hat.

2 Which of the following can you <u>not</u> have on?

  a) a bag   b) earrings   c) make-up   d) your hair   e) a uniform   f) a watch

GRAMMAR
Which of these are grammatically possible?
  a) He had a tie on.
  b) He had on a tie.
  c) He had it on.
  d) He had on it.
  e) The tie was had on.

Now check your answers by looking at *have sth on; have got sth on* on p. 105.

PRACTISE

I Only <u>one</u> of these sentences is grammatically correct. Which one? Can
  you find and correct the mistakes in the other sentences?
  a) Today I'm having my favourite sweater on.
  b) Did she have anything nice on when you saw her?
  c) I was cold because I hadn't a coat on.

2 Answer these questions, using *have something on* or *have got something on*:
  a) What are you wearing now?

  ....

  b) What was your mother wearing last time you saw her?

  ....

Now check your answers by looking at *have sth on; have got sth on* on p. 105.

BUILD YOUR VOCABULARY

OTHER MEANINGS
This verb has two other meanings:
I'm cold. Can we have the heating on? (= Can we have the heating switched on?)
Have you got anything on tomorrow? (= Do you have anything planned or arranged?)

HOLD ON

STUDY Read these sentences carefully.

- **Hold on** a minute. I need to get my coat.
- Can you **hold on**? I'll see if Mr Jones is free to take your call.
- Let's **hold on** for a few minutes and see if anyone else is coming.
- **Hold on** a second! That doesn't sound right at all.

CHECK Use the sentences in the Study box to help you do these exercises.

MEANING

If you ask somebody to *hold on*, what do you want them to do? Choose <u>one</u> answer.

a) stop what they are doing   **b)** wait for a short time

c) hold something

GRAMMAR

Which of these are grammatically possible?
a) Hold on.
b) Hold on the phone.
c) We held on for a few minutes.
d) We were held on for a few minutes.

Now check your answers by looking at *hold on* on p. 105.

PRACTISE

1 In which of these situations would you <u>not</u> ask somebody to *hold on*?
  a) when you want the person on the telephone to wait
  b) when you are in a hurry and somebody is being too slow
  c) when you need to think about the answer to a question

2 What could you say in the following situations? Use *hold on* in each answer.
  a) Your friend is ready to go out, but you need to make a quick phone call.

  ....

  b) The lesson is due to start, but only half the class has arrived. You think it's better if you wait to see if more students arrive.

  ....

Now check your answers by looking at *hold on* on p. 105.

BUILD YOUR VOCABULARY

SYNONYMS

The verb **hang on** means the same and is used in the same way, especially in British English:

Hang on, I'll be with you in a minute.
*Can you **hang on**? I'll see if he's in.*

LOG ON; LOG ONTO *something*

STUDY Read these sentences carefully.

- Can you show me how to **log on**?
- Close all programs and **log on** as a different user.
- I don't know how to **log onto** this machine.
- It's a great website and hundreds of people are **logging onto** it every day.

CHECK Use the sentences in the Study box to help you do these exercises.

MEANING

Choose the best word to complete the meaning of *log on*:

begin   continue   stop

to perform the actions that allow you to .... using a computer system

GRAMMAR

Which of these are grammatically possible?
a) I logged on.
b) I logged the computer on.
c) I logged onto the computer.
d) I logged it on.
e) I logged onto it.

This verb is also common in the pattern **he logged on**: *You are now **logged on**.*

Now check your answers by looking at *log on; log onto sth* on p. 106.

PRACTISE

Complete these sentences with the correct form of *log on* or *log onto* something. Use the objects below where necessary:

the system   the Internet

a) Every evening she .... to check the news.
b) You can't .... without a user name and password.
c) Press CTRL + ALT + DELETE to ....

Now check your answers by looking at *log on; log onto sth* on p. 106.

BUILD YOUR VOCABULARY

RELATED WORDS
noun: **a logon**
*All successful **logons** are recorded.*

SYNONYMS
Log in, **log into something** has the same meaning and is used in the same variety of patterns:
*Will you show me how to **log in**?*
There is also the noun **login**, with the same meaning as **logon**.

OPPOSITES
➤ **log off; log off something**

45

PUT *something* ON

STUDY Read these sentences carefully.

- **Put** a clean shirt **on** before dinner, please.
- He had a shower and **put on** a new black T-shirt.
- She took a pair of dark glasses out of her pocket and **put** them **on**.

CHECK Use the sentences in the Study box to help you do these exercises.

MEANING

1 Which is the best explanation of this meaning of *put something on*?
   a) to be wearing an item of clothing
   b) to put an item of clothing on your body

2 Which of the following can you <u>not</u> *put on*?
   a) shoes   b) a handkerchief   c) a watch   d) earrings   e) an umbrella

GRAMMAR

Which of these are grammatically possible?
   a) He put his coat on.
   b) He put on his coat.
   c) He put it on.
   d) He put on it.
   e) His coat was put on.

Now check your answers by looking at *put sth on* **on p. 107.**

PRACTISE

1 *Put on or wear?* Choose the best verb. The answer to **MEANING** exercise 1 will help you.
   a) Do you *put on / wear* glasses?
   b) What was he *putting on / wearing* when you last saw him?
   c) I got up quickly and *put on / wore* my clothes.

2 Respond to the following, using *put something on* and the object in brackets.
   a) 'I'm very cold!' 'Why don't ....?' *(your jacket)*
   b) 'I've got a job interview this afternoon.' 'Don't forget ....' *(a tie)*

Now check your answers by looking at *put sth on* **on p. 107.**

BUILD YOUR VOCABULARY

OPPOSITES
➤ **take something off**

OTHER MEANINGS
Put something on is also used when you apply cream, perfume, etc. to your skin:
*She spends a long time **putting on** her make-up.*
➤ **turn something on**

TURN *something* ON

STUDY Read these sentences carefully.

- It's a bit dark in here. Shall I **turn** the light **on**?
- Can I **turn on** the television? I want to watch the news.
- I don't understand this machine. How do you **turn** it **on**?
- The heating has **been turned on**, so our offices are nice and warm.

CHECK Use the sentences in the Study box to help you do these exercises.

MEANING

Complete this meaning of *turn something on* using the words below:

electricity   button   start   switch

to .... the flow of ...., gas or water by moving a ....

or pressing a ....

GRAMMAR

Which of these are grammatically possible?

a) He turned the TV on.
b) He turned on the TV.
c) He turned it on.
d) He turned on it.
e) The TV was turned on.

Now check your answers by looking at *turn sth on* on p. 109.

PRACTISE

1 **Complete these sentences in an appropriate way, using a form of** *turn on* **and an object:**

a) It's quite cold in here, isn't it? We ....
b) My computer's broken. It crashes every time I ....
c) She was bored, driving down the motorway on her own, so she

....

2 **Correct any errors in the following:**

a) I forgot to turn the answer machine when I left the house this morning.
b) If you want a hot bath later, you'll have to turning the hot water on now.
c) How can you read in this light? Let me turn on the big light on for you.
d) To turn the power back on, press the standby button.

Now check your answers by looking at *turn sth on* on p. 109.

BUILD YOUR VOCABULARY

OPPOSITES
➤ **turn something off**

SIMILAR VERBS
➤ **turn something up** and **turn something down**

CHECK OUT; CHECK OUT OF *something*

STUDY Read these sentences carefully.

- We have to **check out** by 10 a.m.
- It was nearly twelve by the time she **checked out of** the Hilton.
- He **checked out of** the hospital against his doctor's orders.

CHECK Use the sentences in the Study box to help you do these exercises.

MEANING

1 If you *check out of a hotel*, which of the following do you do? More than one answer is correct.
   a) You visit the hotel.
   b) You pay your bill.
   c) You ask the receptionist questions.
   d) You give back your key.
   e) You leave.

2 Which of these places can you *check out of*?
   a) a hotel   **b)** a motel   **c)** an office   **d)** a hospital
   e) an airport

GRAMMAR
Which of these are grammatically possible?
   a) I checked out.
   b) I checked out the hotel.
   c) I checked out of the hotel.
   d) The hotel was checked out of.

Now check your answers by looking at *check out; check out of sth* on p. 102.

PRACTISE

Complete the sentences with the correct form of *check out* or *check out of*:
   a) What time do I have to .... in the morning?
   b) We .... our hotel early, and went to the airport.
   c) Make sure you haven't left anything in your room before you ....
   d) I tried to find him, but he'd already ....
   e) He called to say that he .... the hospital already.

Now check your answers by looking at *check out; check out of sth* on p. 102.

BUILD YOUR VOCABULARY

RELATED WORDS
noun: **checkout** *(This is an uncountable noun.)*
Checkout *is 11 a.m.*

OPPOSITES
➤ **check in; check somebody or something in**

CHECK *somebody or something* OUT

STUDY Read these sentences carefully.

- The police are **checking out** her story.
- They always **check** people **out** before offering them a job.
- I gave them a false address but they didn't **check** it **out**.
- You need to **get** that cough **checked out** by a doctor.

CHECK Use the sentences in the Study box to help you do these exercises.

MEANING

Complete the meanings, using all of the words below:

honest   true   correct   reliable   acceptable

a) If you check somebody out, you find out if they are ....,
................................, etc.

b) If you check something out, you find out if it is ...., ... or
....

GRAMMAR

Which of these are grammatically possible?

a) I checked his story out.
b) I checked out his story.
c) I checked it out.
d) I checked out it.
e) His story was checked out.

Now check your answers by looking at *check sb/sth out* on p. 102.

PRACTISE

Rewrite the following sentences so that the meaning stays the same,
using the verb *check somebody or something out*:

a) I don't trust him. I think we should find out if his story is true.
   I think we ....

b) The police investigated the names and addresses to see if they were real.
   ....

c) Can you see if something is correct for me?
   ....?

d) They always do thorough checks on any potential employees.
   Potential employees are always ....

Now check your answers by looking at *check sb/sth out* on p. 102.

BUILD YOUR VOCABULARY

OTHER MEANINGS

In informal language, **check somebody or something out** can also mean 'to
look at somebody or something because they or it seem interesting or attractive':
*We're going to **check out** that new bar in town. Do you want to come?*

FIND OUT; FIND *something* OUT

Read these sentences carefully.

- I don't know the answer to that question, but I'll **find out** for you.
- You'll never **find out** my secret!
- How did you **find** that **out**?
- They called him to **find out** why he wasn't at work.
- She was furious when she **found out** that he'd been lying to her.
- Did you **find out** anything about the family?

CHECK Use the sentences in the Study box to help you do these exercises.

MEANING
Which of these verbs can mean the same as *find out*? Choose <u>one</u> answer.

a) to discover   **b)** to invent   **c)** to know

GRAMMAR
Which of these are grammatically possible?
a) I found out.
b) I found the truth out.
c) I found out the truth.
d) I found it out.
e) I found out it.

Now check your answers by looking at *find out; find sth out* on p. 103.

PRACTISE

Find out is often used with question words. Imagine you are a private detective, and a client has asked you to investigate a man who has been following her. She wants the answers to these questions. **Complete the sentences below each question.**

a) (Who is he?)
   I want you to find out who ....

b) (Where does he live?)
   Can you find out where ....?

c) (When did he start following me?)
   Please find out when ....

d) (Why is he following me?)
   I must find out ....

e) (How does he know my name?)
   I need to ....

f) (What does he want?)
   I have to ....

Now check your answers by looking at *find out; find sth out* on p. 103.

DOWN

On pages 8 to 16 you studied these verbs in combination with DOWN:

break   cut   let   put   settle   slow   turn   write

On pages 8 to 16 you studied these verbs in combination with DOWN:

PATTERNS OF MEANING

EXERCISE 1

You may now be able to see some patterns of meaning of verbs that combine with DOWN. The verbs you have studied have two main areas of meaning. Try to fit the verbs in the box into the two categories. You can look back at pages 8 – 16 to help you.

| break down | cut down | let sb down | slow down |
| turn sb/sth down | turn sth down | | |

Failing	Reducing

RELATED WORDS

EXERCISE 2

Complete each sentence with a noun or an adjective related to one of the verbs in the box.

| break down | let sb down | slow down | break down |

a) Many movie stars are a bit of a .... when you meet them.

b) There was an old .... truck by the side of the road.

c) There has been a .... in the world economy.

d) Most delays are caused by accidents, roadworks or vehicle ....

TEST YOURSELF

EXERCISE 3

Now try to complete these sentences with one of the verbs in the correct form.

a) I drink far too much coffee. I really should ...., down.

b) Can you .... your CD player down? I can't get to sleep.

c) I think my daughter is far too young to get married and .... down.

d) The car couldn't .... down in time and crashed into a tree.

e) If you fail this exam again, you'll be .... the whole family down.

f) You'll break that vase! .... it down!

g) She was .... down for the job because of her age.

Check your answers on page R11.

OFF

On pages 22 to 37 you studied these verbs used in combination with OFF:

cut   drop   get   go   log   put   set   take   tell   turn

PATTERNS OF MEANING

EXERCISE 1

You may now be able to see some patterns of meaning of verbs that combine with OFF. There are three main areas of meaning. Try to fit the verbs in the box into the three categories. You can look back at pages 22 – 37 to help you.

cut sb off	cut sb/sth off (meaning 2)	drop sb/sth off
get off, get off sth	log off, log off sth	put sth off
put sb off (meanings 1,2)	set off take off	turn sth off

Departing/leaving	Ending	Stopping/preventing

OPPOSITES

EXERCISE 2

Give the opposites of the phrasal verbs in these sentences.

a) I'll drop you off at your hotel.

b) Where do we get off the bus?

c) Don't forget to log off when you have finished using the computer.

d) The plane took off at 12.20.

e) Would you like to take your coat off?

f) I'll turn the lights off.

EXERCISE 3

Match the phrasal verbs in these sentences with their single word synonyms.

a) Don't stand there watching me – you're putting me off.
b) Let's put the meeting off until next week.
c) We set off at midday.
d) Can you take your boots off before you come indoors?

remove   distract   leave   postpone

EXERCISE 4

Complete the following sentences with a noun or an adjective related to the phrasal verbs in the box.

tell somebody off	put somebody off	take off

a) Do not use mobile phones during .... and landing.
b) I got a terrible .... from Mum!
c) I find her manner very ....

EXERCISE 5

Now test your knowledge of these verbs by completing these sentences with a verb in the correct form. Try to do this without looking back at the pages of individual verbs.

a) My father was so ill we had to .... off the wedding until he was better.
b) The terrible smell in the room .... me off my food.
c) The last person to leave should .... off all the lights.
d) Ask the driver to .... you off at the supermarket.
e) The bus stopped, but no one .... off.
f) The water supply to the house had .... off.
g) I .... the boys off for making so much noise.
h) I think the milk's .... off.
i) The town had .... off by the floods.

Check your answers on page R11.

OUT

On pages 48 to 66 you studied these verbs used in combination with OUT:

check	find	get	give	go	leave
put	run	sell	sort	wear	work

PATTERNS OF MEANING

EXERCISE 1

You may now be able to see some patterns of meaning of verbs that combine with OUT. There are three main areas of meaning. Try to fit the verbs in the box into the three categories. You can look back at pages 48 - 66 to help you.

check out, check out of sth	check sb/sth out	find out, find sth out
get out, get out of sth	go out (meaning 1,3)	put sth out
run out, run out of sth	sell out, sell out of sth, be sold out	
sort sth out	wear out, wear sth out	wear sb/yourself out
work out	work sth out	

Finishing/ending	Leaving/going outside	Solving

SYNONYMS AND OPPOSITES

EXERCISE 2

Use one of the verbs below in a suitable form to complete the comments:

get in	give out	come on	go out	work out	check out

a) Shall we stay in tonight?
   No, let's..........................

b) The lights...........................
   I hope they come on again soon.

c) I just couldn't figure out what he was doing.
   No, I couldn't...........................either.

d) I've got a lot of papers to hand out.
   Shall I help you...........................?

e) You can check in any time after 2 p.m.
   When should we...........................?

EXERCISE 3

Rewrite each sentence using a noun or an adjective formed from the verb in brackets.

a) Every ticket for the concert had been sold.
The concert was .... (SELL OUT)

b) His shoes were old and had large holes in them.
His shoes were .... (WEAR OUT)

c) He hates parties and he's looking for an excuse not to go.
He hates parties and he's .... (GET OUT OF STH)

d) I'm so tired! I've cleaned the whole house today.
.... *I've cleaned the whole house today!* (WEAR OUT)

EXERCISE 4

Choose the best verb to fit in the spaces in these sentences:

a) I'd love some tea, but I don't want to .... you out at all.
    leave   sort   put

b) We can't have any coffee – the milk's .... out.
    sold   run   gone

c) You can't smoke in here. Can you .... your cigarette out, please?
    put   leave   check

d) I wish I could .... out of the meeting. I'm so busy.
    check   get   go

e) Do you believe his story? Perhaps we should .... it out.
    find   check   sort

f) I've cleaned the whole apartment today. It has .... me out.
    put   sorted   worn

g) Dave was upset he was .... out of the team.
    put   left   got

h) The tickets for the concert are all .... out.
    sold   run   gone

i) How long will it take to .... out the problem?
    check   work   sort

j) Can you .... out the answer to number 2?
    check   work   leave

Check your answers on page R11.

UP

On pages 71 - 100 you studied these verbs used in combination with UP:

be	blow	break	bring	catch	cheer	do
fill	get	give	grow	hang	hold	keep
look	make	own	pick	put	set	speak
take	turn	wake				

PATTERNS OF MEANING

EXERCISE 1

You may now be able to see some patterns of meaning of verbs that combine with UP. There are three main areas of meaning. Put the verbs in the box into the three catagories. You can look back at pages 71 – 100 to help you.

blow sth up	break up	bring sb up
cheer up, cheer sb/yourself up	fill sth up	
give up, give up sth (meaning 1,2)	grow up	hang up, hang up sth
hold sb/sth up	speak up	turn sth up
wake up, wake sb up		

Increasing/improving	Stopping/delaying	Completing/finishing

OPPOSITES

EXERCISE 2

Match the phrasal verbs in these sentences with their opposites in the box.

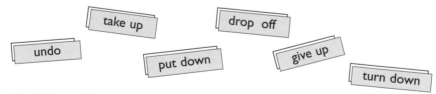

take up   drop off   undo   put down   give up   turn down

a) When did you give up smoking?

b) He had difficulty doing up the buttons on his coat.

c) Can you turn up the heating a bit?

d) I'll pick you up at your house.

e) She picked the vase up carefully.

f) I've decided to take up line dancing.

RELATED WORDS

EXERCISE 3

Complete the sentences with a noun or an adjective formed from the verb in brackets.

a) George had a very strict .... (BRING UP)

b) .... are expected because of roadworks at the junction. (HOLD UP)

c) It isn't a true story. It's a .... one. (MAKE UP)

d) What time would you like your .... call? (WAKE UP)

e) It took him a long time to recover from the .... of his marriage. (BREAK UP)

f) There's a bus .... point in front of the hotel. (PICK UP)

g) .... on this site are free and easy to use. (LOOK UP)

TEST YOURSELF

EXERCISE 4

The phrasal verbs in these sentences have been mixed up so that the wrong one is in each sentence. Rearrange the verbs so that each sentence has the correct verb.

a) I didn't like your boss. I don't know how you caught up with him.

b) Julia was late again today. I think the traffic picked her up.

c) I didn't know the answer to the question so I owned one up.

d) He was so rude! When he heard my voice on the phone he just cheered up!

e) Who broke the window? Will someone hang up?

f) The rest of the group were still so far ahead I knew Jack hadn't put up with them.

g) Dan looked so miserable but I held him up.

h) I made up the kids from school this afternoon.

EXERCISE 5

Rewrite these sentences, replacing the noun or phrase in italics with a pronoun in the correct position.

a) How do you put up with *that noise* all the time?
   How do you ....?

b) When did you take up *judo*?
   When did you ....?

c) I decided not to look up *the words* in a dictionary.
   I decided not to ....

d) I'm sure he made up *that story*.
   I'm sure ....

Check your answers on page R12

OTHER PARTICLES

In this book you have studied verbs combining with other particles, including:

away	in	on	over

PATTERNS OF MEANING

EXERCISE 1

You may be able to see the main areas of meaning of these particles in the verbs you have studied. Put each verb in the box in the correct category in the table. You can look back at the relevant verb pages to help you.

throw sth away	go on (meaning 1)	log on, log onto sth
give sth away	get on, get on sth	get in, get in sth
turn sth on	turn over, turn sb/sth over	

Movement in a particular direction	Removing	Continuing	Starting

TEST YOURSELF

EXERCISE 2

Choose the best verb to fit into the spaces in these sentences:

a) ……………….. on. I'll just get some paper to write all that down.

   come　　**turn**　　**hold**

b) Shall we ……………….. in before we have a cup of coffee?

   check　　**fill**　　**log**

c) Put your shoes on properly or you'll ……………….over.

   get　　**turn**　　**fall**

d) It took him a long time to …………….. over his illness.

   fall　　**get**　　**throw**

e) Can you describe what she …………. on when you last saw her?

   got　　**held**　　**had**

f) Please ……………..in your full name and your address.

   log　　**fill**　　**turn**

Check your answers on page R12.

GET

GET can be used in combination with a variety of adverbs and prepositions. In this book you have met GET in combination with:

in	**off**	**on**	**out**	**over**	**up**

MEANING

EXERCISE 1

Match each sentence with an explanation of the meaning in the box.

a) I'm still getting over my cold.

b) They were locked in the building and couldn't get out.

c) It's 6.30! You should be getting up now.

d) Jack got in the car and drove off.

e) Do you get on well with your teachers?

f) I said I would go shopping with him, so I can't get out of it now.

g) Anna got off the bus and started to walk along the road.

h) We had to break a window to get in.

i)	to get into a bus, train, plane, car, etc.
ii)	to have a friendly relationship with somebody
iii)	to manage to find a way out of a place
iv)	to return to your usual state of health or happiness after an illness, a shock, etc.
v)	to get out of bed
vi)	to leave a bus, train or plane
vii)	to succeed in entering a place
viii)	to avoid a responsibility or duty

TEST YOURSELF

EXERCISE 2

The phrasal verbs in these sentences have been mixed up so that the wrong one is in each sentence. Rearrange the verbs so that each sentence has the correct verb.

a) My parents don't get over their neighbours very well.

b) Don't leave your bags on the train when you get on it.

c) You promised to help me! You can't get off it now.

d) I watched him get up his bike and ride away.

e) Come on, lazy! It's time to get in.

f) Be quick and get on with the car! We're late.

g) I was very angry with him, but he'll get out of it.

Check your answers on page R12.

PUT

PUT can be used in combination with a variety of adverbs and prepositions. In this book you have met PUT in combination with:

away   down   off   on   out   up   with

MEANING

EXERCISE 1

Match each sentence with an explanation of the meaning in the box.

a) It's cold outside – you'll need to put on a coat.
b) I'd love some tea, but I don't want to put you out at all.
c) How do you put up with all that noise?
d) Don't watch me – you're putting me off!
e) He washed the dishes and put them away.
f) She put her bag down by the door.
g) The fire was put out before the firefighters arrived.
h) We'll have to put the meeting off until next week.
i) The accident put her off driving for years.

i)   to put something in a box, a drawer, etc. because you have finished using it
ii)   to change something to a later date or time
iii)   to make somebody stop liking something
iv)   to accept something that is annoying or unpleasant without complaining
v)   to place something that you are holding on the floor
vi)   to make trouble, problems or extra work for somebody
vii)   to put an item of clothing on your body
viii) to stop something burning
ix)   to disturb somebody who is trying to give their attention to something

TEST YOURSELF

EXERCISE 2

Complete the dialogues in an appropriate way, using a phrasal verb with PUT and anything else that you need.

a) Would you like to stay the night here?
   Oh, I don't want ....

b) My car broke down again the other day!
   I don't know why...

c) Do you like strong cheese?
   No, it's the smell that.....................................

d) It feels a bit cold in here.
   Why don't you.......................................?

Check your answers on page R12.

DOWN

Exercise 1

Failing: break down; let sb down; turn sb/sth down

Reducing: cut down; slow down; turn sth down

Exercise 2

a) let-down **b)** broken-down **c)** slowdown **d)** breakdowns

Exercise 3

a) cut **b)** turn **c)** settle **d)** slow **e)** letting **f)** Put **g)** turned

OFF

Exercise 1

Departing and leaving: drop sb/sth off; get off, get off sth; set off; take off

Ending: cut sb off; cut sb/sth off; log off, log off sth; turn sth off

Stopping/preventing: put sth off; put sb off (1,2)

Exercise 2

a) pick up **b)** get on **c)** log on **d)** land **e)** put on **f)** turn on

Exercise 3

a) distract **b)** postpone **c)** leave **d)** remove

Exercise 4

a) take-off **b)** telling-off **c)** off-putting

Exercise 5

a) put **b)** put **c)** turn **d)** drop **e)** got **f)** been cut **g)** told
h) gone **i)** been cut

OUT

Exercise 1

Finishing/ending: go out (3); put sth out; run out, run out of sth; sell out, sell out of sth; be sold out; wear out, wear sth out; wear sb/yourself out; work out

Leaving/going outside: check out, check out of sth; get out, get out of sth; go out (1)

Solving: check sb/sth out; find out, find sth out; sort sth out; work sth out

Exercise 2

a) No, let's go out. **b)** The lights have gone out. **c)** No, I couldn't work it out either.
d) Shall I help you give them out? **e)** When should we check out?

Exercise 3

a) a sell-out **b)** worn out **c)** looking for a get-out **d)** I'm worn out

Exercise 4

a) put **b)** run **c)** put **d)** get **e)** check **f)** worn **g)** left **h)** sold **i)** sort **j)** work

UP

Exercise 1

Increasing/improving: blow sth up; bring sb up; cheer up, cheer sb/yourself up; grow up; speak up; turn sth up

Stopping/delaying: break up; give up, give sth up (1,2); hang up, hang up sth; hold sb/sth up

Completing/finishing: fill sth up; wake up, wake sb up

Exercise 2

a) take up **b)** undo **c)** turn down **d)** drop off **e)** put down **f)** give up

Exercise 3

a) upbringing **b)** hold-ups **c)** made-up **d)** wake-up **e)** break-up **f)** pickup **g)** look-ups

Exercise 4

a) put up with him **b)** held her up **c)** made one up **d)** hung up **e)** own up
f) caught up with them **g)** cheered him up **h)** picked up the kids

Exercise 5

a) put up with it **b)** take it up **c)** look them up **d)** he made it up

OTHER PARTICLES

Exercise 1

Movement in a particular direction: get on, get on sth; get in, get in sth; turn over, turn sb/sth over

Removing: throw sth away; give sth away

Continuing: go on (1)

Starting: log on, log onto sth; turn sth on

Exercise 2

a) Hold **b)** check **c)** fall **d)** get **e)** had **f)** fill

GET

Exercise 1

a) iv **b)** iii **c)** v **d)** i **e)** ii **f)** viii **g)** vi **h)** vii

Exercise 2

a) get on with **b)** get off it **c)** get out of it **d)** get on **e)** get up
f) get in **g)** get over it

PUT

Exercise 1

a) vii **b)** vi **c)** iv **d)** ix **e)** i **f)** v **g)** viii **h)** ii **i)** iii

Exercise 2

Suggested answers:

a) Oh I don't want to put you out (at all).
b) I don't know why you put up with it.
c) No, it's the smell that puts me off.
d) Why don't you put your sweater on?

GET OUT; GET OUT OF *something*

STUDY Read these sentences carefully.

- The driver's door opened and an elderly woman **got out**.
- The doors and windows were locked and they couldn't **get out**.
- I didn't **get out of** bed until after ten o'clock.
- The car was very small, but six people **got out of** it.
- I'm scared. Let's **get out of** here.

CHECK Use the sentences in the Study box to help you do these exercises.

MEANING

1 *Get out* usually means 'to leave or go out'. Which of the following can you get out of?
a) a car   **b)** a bicycle   **c)** a train   **d)** a building   **e)** a room
f) a chair   **g)** home

2 Which of the following is closest in meaning to the sentence *They got out of the building*?
a) They had to leave the building.
b) They tried to leave the building.
c) They managed to leave the building.

GRAMMAR
Which of these are grammatically possible?
a) I got out.
b) I got out of the car.
c) I got it out.
d) I got out of it.
e) The car was got out of.

Now check your answers by looking at *get out; get out of sth* on p. 103.

PRACTISE

Complete these sentences with the correct form of *get out* or *get out of*. Use the objects below <u>where necessary</u>:
here   the office
a) It was crowded, but then lots of people .... at the next station.
b) Somehow the cat had climbed into the box and it couldn't ....
c) Let's .... We can walk the rest of the way.
d) I usually try to .... for an hour at lunchtime.

Now check your answers by looking at *get out; get out of sth* on p. 103.

BUILD YOUR VOCABULARY

OPPOSITES
➤ **get in; get in something**

SIMILAR VERBS
The verb **get off; get off something** has a similar meaning.

51

GET OUT OF *something*

STUDY Read these sentences carefully.

- I wish I could **get out of** this meeting! I'm so busy.
- He'd promised to go out with some colleagues and he couldn't **get out of** it.
- The wedding's all arranged. There's no **getting out of** it now.
- She's not really ill; she's just trying to **get out of** taking the English test.

CHECK Use the sentences in the Study box to help you do these exercises.

MEANING
Which of the following is <u>not</u> an explanation of the meaning of *get out of something*?
a) to avoid a responsibility or duty
b) to not do something that you ought to do
c) to not do something that you want to do

GRAMMAR
Which of these are grammatically possible?
a) I got out the meeting.
b) I got out of the meeting.
c) I got out of to attend the meeting.
d) I got out of attending the meeting.
e) I got out of it.
f) The meeting was got out of.

Now check your answers by looking at *get out of sth* on p. 104.

PRACTISE

1 You don't want to go to a meeting. Can you *get out of* it? Answer *yes* or *no* for each of the following:
a) Your manager told you to go.
b) No one will mind if you don't go.
c) It's optional.
d) It's compulsory.

2 Complete the following in a suitable way, using *get out of something* or *get out of doing something* and any other necessary information:
a) We promised we'd go to the party - we can't ....
b) He complained that the meal was terrible and tried ....
c) He hated the science classes, but there was ....
d) It's a very important meeting. I don't think I ....

Now check your answers by looking at *get out of sth* on p. 104.

BUILD YOUR VOCABULARY

RELATED WORDS
noun: **a get-out** (= a way of avoiding something) *(This is usually a singular noun.)*
They're looking for an easy **get-out**.

GIVE something OUT

STUDY Read these sentences carefully.

- The conductor is the person on a bus who **gives out** tickets.
- They were standing in the street **giving** leaflets **out** to passers-by.
- We made invitations and **gave** them **out** to our friends.
- The papers **were given out** and we had an hour to do the test.

CHECK Use the sentences in the Study box to help you do these exercises.

MEANING

Which one of these verbs means the same as *give something out?*

a) to collect   **b)** to distribute   **c)** to offer

GRAMMAR

Which of these are grammatically possible?

a) I gave the books out.
b) I gave out the books.
c) I gave them out.
d) I gave out them.
e) The books were given out.

Now check your answers by looking at *give sth out* on p. 104.

PRACTISE

Complete the following with the correct form of *give something out* and one of the objects below. Use each object once only.

free food   leaflets   exam papers   invitations

a) She .... to her wedding to all her colleagues.
b) The teacher asked for silence and started .... to all the students.
c) The relief organizations had arrived and were .... to the refugees.
d) How is the campaign going? Do you need any help with ....?

Now check your answers by looking at *give sth out* on p. 104.

BUILD YOUR VOCABULARY

SYNONYMS

The verb **hand something out** means the same and is used in the same way:
*Can you help me **hand** these books **out**, please?*
*A free factsheet **was handed out** at the end of the session.*

OTHER MEANINGS

Give something out can also mean **1** to produce something such as heat or light:
*That lamp doesn't **give out** a lot of light.*
2 to tell people something or broadcast something:
*No details of the accident have been **given out** yet.*

GO OUT

FIRST MEANING

STUDY Read these sentences carefully.

- We're **going out** for a meal. Do you want to come?
- You look very smart this evening. Are you **going out**?
- He **goes out** a lot.
- Jenny usually **goes out** with her friends on Friday evenings.

CHECK Use the sentences in the Study box to help you do these exercises.

MEANING

Choose the best meaning of this use of *go out*:
a) to leave a building and not return
b) to leave your house to go to a social event
c) to leave one place and go to a different place

GRAMMAR

Which of these are grammatically possible?
a) We went out.
b) We went out the house.
c) We were gone out.

Now check your answers by looking at *go out* **on p. 105.**

PRACTISE

1 Answer the following questions, using *go out* **and the phrases below, with any other necessary information:**

my friends   a party   a special meal
a) Did you celebrate your wedding anniversary?
    Yes, we ....
b) What do you do at weekends?
    I usually ....
c) Is Jim here?
    No, ...

2 Are these sentences true or false for you? If they are false, change the information to make them correct.
a) I always go out on Friday and Saturday evenings.
b) I went out last night.
c) My parents never let me go out when I was young.

Now check your answers by looking at *go out* **on p. 105.**

BUILD YOUR VOCABULARY

OPPOSITES

The opposite of this meaning of **go out** is **stay in**:
*Do you want to **go out** tonight or would you rather **stay in**?*

GO OUT

SECOND MEANING

STUDY Read these sentences carefully.

- They started **going out** together when they were still at school.
- She's **going out** with her best friend's brother.
- How long have you and Anthony been **going out**?
- They **went out** for nearly a year, but they're not together any more.

CHECK Use the sentences in the Study box to help you do these exercises.

MEANING

Use three of the words below to complete this meaning of *go out*:

money   time   relationship   romantic   friendly   poor

to spend .... with somebody and have a ....

.... with them

GRAMMAR

Which of these are grammatically possible?

a) They are going out.
b) They are going out together.
c) He's going out with her.
d) He's going out together.

Go out is often used in the progressive tenses with this meaning.

Now check your answers by looking at *go out* on p. 105.

PRACTISE

1 Rewrite the following sentences so that the meaning stays the same,
using *go out*:

a) Kate and Sam have been boyfriend and girlfriend for three years.

....

b) How long were those two together?

....

c) They had a relationship for years before they finally got married.

....

d) Do you have a boyfriend at the moment?

....

2 Write a sentence about a romantic relationship that you are having
now or that you had in the past, for example:

*I once had a Spanish boyfriend. We went out for nearly a year, but then he went back
to Spain.*

....

Now check your answers by looking at *go out* on p. 105.

GO OUT

THIRD MEANING

Read these sentences carefully.

- There was a power cut and all the lights **went out**.
- Don't let the fire **go out**, please.
- The match **went out**, so he lit another one.

CHECK Use the sentences in the Study box to help you do these exercises.

MEANING
Complete the meanings with a word or phrase from the brackets:
a) If a light goes out, it stops .... *(shining / changing)*
b) If a fire goes out, it stops .... *(spreading / burning)*

GRAMMAR
Which of these are grammatically possible?
a) The lights went out.
b) They went out the lights.
c) The lights were gone out.

Now check your answers by looking at *go out* on p. 105.

PRACTISE

**1 What does *it* refer to in each sentence? Choose from the words below.
Use each object only once.**

the candle   the fire   the flame   the torch

a) I put more wood on it, but it still went out.
b) It flickered, then went out.
c) Don't put it by the window. It'll go out.
d) It keeps going out. Maybe the battery is flat.

**2 Answer these questions in a suitable way, using *go out* and any other
necessary information.**
a) Why is it so cold?

   ....

b) Who turned out the lights?
   Nobody. ....

Now check your answers by looking at *go out* on p. 105.

BUILD YOUR VOCABULARY

OPPOSITES
The opposite of **go out** is **go on** or **come on**:
*We sat in the dark for ten minutes, then the lights suddenly **came on** again.*
*There was a light **going on** and off up ahead in the distance.*

SIMILAR VERBS
➤ **put something out** and **turn something off**

56

LEAVE *somebody or something* **OUT;**
LEAVE *somebody or something* **OUT OF** *something*

STUDY **Read these sentences carefully.**

- You've spelt Michael's name wrong. You've **left out** the 'a'.
- I realized that I'd **left** Jenny **out** and went to get a cup for her.
- Can you check the guest list for me? I don't want to **leave** anyone **out**.
- Why did you decide to **leave** Smith **out of** the team?
- She **was** always **left out** when it was time to make important decisions.

CHECK **Use the sentences in the Study box to help you do these exercises.**

MEANING

1 **What is the** <u>opposite</u> **of** *leave out*? **Choose one answer.**

  a) to add   **b)** to include   **c)** to omit

2 **If you** *leave someone or something out*, **is it...?**
  a) accidental *(= you didn't mean to do it)*
  b) intentional *(= you meant to do it)*
  c) either accidental or intentional

GRAMMAR

  Which of the following are grammatically possible?
  a) I left Alison out.
  b) I left out Alison.
  c) I left her out.
  d) I left out her.
  e) Alison was left out.

Now check your answers by looking at *leave sb/sth out; leave sb/sth out of sth* **on p. 106.**

PRACTISE

  Complete the second sentence so that the meaning stays the same as the first, using a form of *leave out*.
  a) Tell me what happened, and give me all the details!
     Tell me what happened, and don't ....!
  b) It seemed wrong not to invite Daisy, so she came along too.
     It seemed wrong ....
  c) I wrote the number down, but I forgot to write the '0'.
     I wrote the number down, but ....
  d) David wasn't included in the team because of injury.
     David ....
  Now check your answers by looking at *leave sb/sth out; leave sb/sth out of sth* **on p. 106.**

57

PUT *somebody* OUT

STUDY Read these sentences carefully.

- I didn't want to **put** my aunt **out**, so I only stayed one night with her.
- I'd love a cup of tea, if it doesn't **put** you **out** too much.
- Would it **put** your parents **out** if we brought the kids with us?

CHECK Use the sentences in the Study box to help you do these exercises.

MEANING

Which of the following is the best explanation of the meaning of this use of *put somebody out*?

a) to make somebody leave a place or a job
b) to make trouble, problems or extra work for somebody
c) to make somebody angry or annoyed

GRAMMAR

Which of these are grammatically possible?

a) She put her family out.
b) She put out her family.
c) She put them out.
d) She put out them.
e) She put it out.

Now check your answers by looking at *put sb out* on p. 107.

PRACTISE

1 Decide whether somebody or something has *put* the speaker *out* or not, according to what he/she says. Put a tick for *yes*, or a cross for *no*.

a) I'm going into town anyway, so it's no trouble to take Harry to school.
b) He stayed with us for three whole weeks, which was rather difficult.
c) This is the third time I've done this journey today!
d) Jane stayed for dinner, which was lovely.

2 There is a grammatical mistake in <u>each</u> of these sentences. Can you find them and correct them?

a) I hope our arriving late didn't put yourself out at all.
b) Would it put out you too much if he came to stay for a day or two?

Now check your answers by looking at *put sb out* on p. 107.

BUILD YOUR VOCABULARY

OTHER MEANINGS

Put yourself out, meaning 'to make a special effort to do something for somebody ', is also common:
*She really **put herself out** for her visitors.*
In the passive, **be put out** usually means 'be upset or offended':
*He **was** extremely **put out** when I couldn't remember his name.*

PUT *something* OUT

- You can't smoke in here. **Put** that cigarette **out**, please.
- They tried to **put out** the fire themselves.
- The paper caught fire, but thankfully we managed to **put** it **out**.
- It was late at night before the blaze **was** finally **put out**.

CHECK Use the sentences in the Study box to help you do these exercises.

MEANING

Choose one of the words below to complete the meaning of this use of *put something out*:

to stop something ....

a) burning   **b)** shining   **c)** working

GRAMMAR

Which of these are grammatically possible?
a) They put the fire out.
b) They put out the fire.
c) They put it out.
d) They put out it.
e) The fire was put out.

> **Now check your answers by looking at** *put sth out* **on p. 107.**

PRACTISE

1 Match the two halves to make complete sentences:
  a) After more than ten hours   **i)** to put the flames out.
  b) His cigar was making me cough   **ii)** before any serious damage was done.
  c) Fortunately, the fire was put out   **iii)** so he put it out.
  d) Two hose reels were used   **iv)** the fire still hadn't been put out.

2 Complete the following sentences in an appropriate way, using a form of *put out* and any other necessary words or phrases:
  a) It is a firefighter's job to ....
  b) He was smoking in my room, which I hate, so I asked him if

  ....
  c) The blaze destroyed two shops before it ....

> **Now check your answers by looking at** *put sth out* **on p. 107.**

BUILD YOUR VOCABULARY

SYNONYMS

To **extinguish something** has the same meaning as to **put something out**, but is usually more formal:

*All passengers are kindly requested to **extinguish** their cigarettes and fasten their seatbelts.*

RUN OUT; RUN OUT OF *something*

STUDY **Read these sentences carefully.**

- Money **ran out** after four years and the building was never finished.
- 'Why has the car stopped?' 'It's **run out of** petrol.'
- 'Can I have a copy of the handout?' 'I'm afraid we've **run out**.'
- I've **run out of** sugar. I'll see if I can borrow some.
- Time is **running out** and we still have loads to do.

CHECK Use the sentences in the Study box to help you do these exercises.

MEANING

Use three of the words below to complete the meaning of *run out*:

little   none   supply   used

if a supply of something runs out, or if a person runs out of a .... of
something, there is .... left because it has all been ....

GRAMMAR

Which of these are grammatically possible?
a) Our money ran out.
b) We ran out.
c) We ran out money.
d) We ran out of money.
e) Our money was run out of.

Now check your answers by looking at *run out; run out of sth* on p. 108.

PRACTISE

1 **Respond to the following in an appropriate way, using a form of *run out* or *run out of* in each response and any other necessary information:**
a) Why was the project stopped?
   Because funds ....
b) Shall I make us a coffee?
   You can't. We ....
c) Is there any more wine?
   I think it ....
d) Are you going to have another Coke?
   No. I ....

2 **Correct any errors in the following:**
a) The torch doesn't work The battery must have run out.
b) You have run out space on the disk.
c) Dad took so many photos he soon runs out of film.
d) The report was printed on blue paper, as the white had ran out.
e) They ran out of petrol in the middle of nowhere.
f) The whole team is tired and they're running out ideas.

Now check your answers by looking at *run out; run out of sth* on p. 108.

SELL OUT; SELL OUT OF *something*; BE SOLD OUT

STUDY Read these sentences carefully.

- Tickets for the game will **sell out** very quickly.
- 'I'd like some bread, please.' 'I'm afraid we've **sold out**.'
- They had **sold out of** milk by 9 a.m.
- The performance **was** completely **sold out**.
- We **are** already **sold out** for Saturday's concert.

CHECK Use the sentences in the Study box to help you do these exercises.

MEANING
Complete the meanings with a word or phrase from the brackets:
a) If something **sells out**, it is .... *(almost / all)* sold and there is
   .... *(a little / none)* left.
b) If somebody **sells out** or **sells out of** something, they have sold
   .... *(all / most)* of it and have .... *(nothing / little)* left.

GRAMMAR
Which of these are grammatically possible?
a) The tickets sold out.
b) They sold out the tickets.
c) They sold out of tickets.
d) The tickets were sold out.

Now check your answers by looking at *sell out; sell out of sth; be sold out* on p. 108.

PRACTISE

Answer these questions in a suitable way, including a form of *sell out* or *be sold out* in each answer.
a) Did you get the newspaper?
   No, ...
b) Why are you reserving your tickets so early?
   Because ....
c) Do you have this shirt in blue, please?
   I'm afraid ....

Now check your answers by looking at *sell out; sell out of sth; be sold out* on p. 108.

BUILD YOUR VOCABULARY

RELATED WORDS
noun: **a sell-out** (= a show, a football game, etc. for which all the tickets have been sold) *(This is usually a singular noun.)*
*Their concert was a **sell-out**.*

SORT *something* **OUT**

STUDY Read these sentences carefully.

- We have **sorted out** our problems and everything is fine now.
- If the heating breaks down, an engineer will quickly **sort** things **out**.
- There's a crisis at the office and they need me there to **sort** it **out**.
- The system has broken down. It could take days for it to **be sorted out**.

CHECK Use the sentences in the Study box to help you do these exercises.

MEANING

Choose the best word or phrase from the brackets to complete the meaning of *sort something out*:

to .... *(deal with / organize)* a problem or situation in a
.... *(satisfactory / tidy)* way

GRAMMAR

Which of these are grammatically possible?

a) We sorted our problems out.
b) We sorted out our problems.
c) We sorted them out.
d) We sorted out them.
e) Our problems were sorted out.

Now check your answers by looking at *sort sth out* on p. 108.

PRACTISE

Write questions to fit with the following responses, using a form of *sort something out* in each question and one of the objects below:

all the problems   the problem with the heating   your timetable

a) ....?

No I didn't. It still doesn't work properly.

b) ....?

Yes they have. Everything's fine now.

c) ....?

Yes I did. I can go to the Italian classes now.

Now check your answers by looking at *sort sth out* on p. 108.

BUILD YOUR VOCABULARY

OTHER MEANINGS

Sort something out also means 'to put something in order or tidy something':
*We need to **sort out** these papers and file them away.*
It can also mean 'to arrange or organize something':
*He still hasn't **sorted out** accommodation for our stay in Italy.*

WEAR OUT; WEAR *something* OUT

- They are trying to design tyres that do not **wear out**.
- He **wore out** two pairs of boots during one winter.
- Stop pacing up and down. You'll **wear** the carpet **out**!
- She rarely wore the shoes because she didn't want to **wear** them **out**.
- The sofa had **been** completely **worn out** by so many children playing on it.

CHECK Use the sentences in the Study box to help you do these exercises.

MEANING

If something *wears out*, which of the following might be true? More than one answer is correct.

a) it can no longer be used   **b)** it is damaged   **c)** it is old-fashioned

d) it has been used too much

GRAMMAR

Which of these are grammatically possible?

a) His shoes wore out.
b) He wore his shoes out.
c) He wore out his shoes.
d) He wore them out.
e) He wore out them.
f) His shoes had been worn out.

Now check your answers by looking at *wear out; wear sth out* on p. 110.

PRACTISE

1 Complete these sentences, using a suitable form of *wear out* and an object (a noun or a pronoun) <u>where necessary</u>:

a) She takes good care of her clothes. They never seem to ....
b) If you play that videotape too much you ....
c) My son usually grows out of his shoes before ....
d) She made her jeans into a pair of shorts when the knees ....

2 Can you find and correct the mistakes in these sentences?

a) She needed a new pair of shoes because the ones she had were wore out.
b) Even expensive trainers wear them out and have to be replaced.
c) He walks a lot and says he wears out two pairs of shoes out a year.

Now check your answers by looking at *wear out; wear sth out* on p. 110.

BUILD YOUR VOCABULARY

RELATED WORDS

adjective: **worn out**
*These trousers are **worn out**. I need some new ones.*
*He was wearing a pair of old **worn-out** trainers.*

WEAR *somebody or yourself* OUT

STUDY Read these sentences carefully.

- She **wore** her parents **out** by refusing to go to bed every night.
- The kids have **worn** me **out**.
- You'll **wear** yourself **out** if you carry on working so hard.

CHECK Use the sentences in the Study box to help you do these exercises.

MEANING

If something *wears you out,* how do you feel? Choose <u>one</u> answer.

a) very bored   **b)** very ill   **c)** very old   **d)** very tired

GRAMMAR

Which of these are grammatically possible?

a) She wore out.
b) She wore her parents out.
c) She wore out her parents.
d) She wore them out.
e) She wore out them.
f) She wore herself out.

Now check your answers by looking at *wear sb/yourself out* on p. 110.

PRACTISE

1 **Complete these sentences with a suitable form of *wear out* and one of the objects below:**

him   himself   me   you   yourself

a) If you ask me, he works too hard. He'll ....
b) Can we go home now? All that shopping ....
c) You look tired. Did the journey ....?
d) Why don't you go home and rest? There's no point ....
e) He's in bed already. I think the kids ....

2 **Complete this sentence in a suitable way, using this verb.**

I'm not going out tonight. I ....!

Now check your answers by looking at *wear sb/yourself out* on p. 110.

BUILD YOUR VOCABULARY

RELATED WORDS

adjective: **worn out** *(This does not usually come before a noun.)*
Come and sit down. You look **worn out***!*
I went home feeling **worn out** *after the conference.*

WORK OUT

STUDY Read these sentences carefully.

- My mother is living with us now, which is **working out** well.
- I do hope things **work out** for him. He deserves to be happy.
- Unfortunately, their marriage didn't **work out** and they got divorced last year.
- My trip to London didn't **work out** the way I'd planned.

CHECK Use the sentences in the Study box to help you do these exercises.

MEANING

Use <u>three</u> of the words below to complete this meaning of *work out*:

successful   way   happen   become

to .... or develop in a particular ....,

especially in a .... way

GRAMMAR

Which of these are grammatically possible?
a) Things worked out.
b) We worked out things.
c) Things worked themselves out.

Now check your answers by looking at *work out* on p. 110.

PRACTISE

1 In <u>two</u> of these sentences the verb *work out* is not used correctly. Can you find which ones and correct the mistakes?
   a) Laura and Pete were married for five years, but they didn't work out.
   b) I knew I could always go back home if it didn't work out at the new flat.
   c) Will you call me and let me know how things work out?
   d) We needn't have worried. Everything didn't work out really well.

2 Answer the following question in two different ways, one positive and one negative, using a form of *work out* in each answer.
   How is Liz getting on in her new job?
   a) ....
   b) ....

   Now check your answers by looking at *work out* on p. 110.

BUILD YOUR VOCABULARY

OTHER MEANINGS

If a person **works out**, they train their body by physical exercise:
*I try to **work out** in the gym three times a week.*
*You look well. Have you been **working out**?*
A very common related noun is **a workout**:
*I did a two-hour **workout** in the gym.*

WORK *something* OUT

STUDY Read these sentences carefully.

- We need to **work out** the total cost of the project before we agree to it.
- It took him two days to **work** the code **out**.
- Don't tell me the answer. I want to **work** it **out** for myself.
- I can't **work out** how you got here so quickly.
- Any reductions will **be worked out** before you receive your bill.

CHECK Use the sentences in the Study box to help you do these exercises.

MEANING

1 Which of the following means the same as *to work out the total*?
- **a)** to decide on the total
- **b)** to calculate the total

2 *Work something out* also means 'to find the answer to a question or something that is difficult to understand or explain'. Which of these can you *work out*?
- **a)** the rules of a game
- **b)** the news
- **c)** how to operate the washing machine

GRAMMAR

Which of these are grammatically possible?
- **a)** He worked the figures out.
- **b)** He worked out the figures.
- **c)** He worked them out.
- **d)** He worked out them.
- **e)** The figures were worked out.

Now check your answers by looking at *work sth out* on p. 110.

PRACTISE

1 Correct any grammatical errors in the following:
- **a)** It took me a long time to work out the grammar of phrasal verbs out.
- **b)** I am very bad at working sums out in my head. I have to write them down.
- **c)** I think it's fun to working out mathematical problems and other puzzles.

2 Can you work these puzzles out?
- **a)** How many times does the number 3 appear between 1 and 50?
- **b)** What gets wetter as it dries?

Now check your answers by looking at *work sth out* on p. 110.

BUILD YOUR VOCABULARY

SYNONYMS

The verb **figure something out** means the same and is used in the same way:
*I can't **figure out** what's gone wrong.*

FALL OVER

STUDY Read these sentences carefully.

- I'm afraid that he might **fall over** again and hurt himself.
- She still can't walk properly - she keeps **falling over**.
- I just touched the vase and it **fell over**.

CHECK Use the sentences in the Study box to help you do these exercises.

MEANING
Complete the meaning of *fall over* with a phrase from the brackets:
to be unable to *(stay standing / get up)* and *(lie on / fall to)* the ground

GRAMMAR
Which of these are grammatically possible?
a) I fell over.
b) I fell over the ground.
c) I fell myself over.
d) The bicycle fell over.
e) The bicycle fell over it.

Now check your answers by looking at *fall over* on p. 103.

PRACTISE

1 Which of the following would be logical answers to this question?
　　Why did you fall over?
a) I was sitting down.
b) My foot slipped.
c) I suddenly felt very dizzy.
d) I was holding on to the wall.

2 Which <u>three</u> of these objects are the most likely to *fall over*?
a) a large pile of books on a table
b) an old car on a flat road
c) a tall tree in a storm
d) a chair with a broken leg
e) the wheel of a bike

Now check your answers by looking at *fall over* on p. 103.

BUILD YOUR VOCABULARY

SIMILAR VERBS
If you **fall over something** you hit something with your foot when you are
walking or running, and fall or almost fall:
*She **fell over** a chair as she was trying to escape.*
*You'd better move this box or somebody will **fall over** it.*
Fall down has a similar meaning to **fall over**:
*If we don't repair the wall, it might **fall down**.*

GET OVER *somebody or something*

STUDY **Read these sentences carefully.**

- He didn't go out as he was still **getting over** the flu.
- Once he'd **got over** the shock of seeing me again, we had a good time.
- I loved Mark very much. It took me a long time to **get over** him.
- My pride was hurt, but I'll **get over** it.
- He says he'll never **get over** losing her.

CHECK Use the sentences in the Study box to help you do these exercises.

MEANING

1 Which of the following is closest in meaning to this use of *get over* somebody or something? Choose <u>one</u> answer.

a) to climb over   **b)** to recover from   **c)** to return from

2 Which <u>two</u> of these can you get over?

a) a shock   **b)** a new job   **c)** a cold
d) a wedding

GRAMMAR

Which of these are grammatically possible?
a) I got the illness over.
b) I got over the illness.
c) I got it over.
d) I got over it.

Now check your answers by looking at *get over sb/sth* on p. 104.

PRACTISE

Complete the following sentences with an appropriate form of *get over* and one of the phrases below:

it now   the long flight   bronchitis   the shock   her homesickness

a) It was the first time she'd been away from her family, but she soon

....

b) I couldn't join in with the singing, as I ....

c) When ...., I started to make plans to spend my £1 million prize.

d) He was very ill, but he seems to ....

e) We spent the first day of our holiday ....

Now check your answers by looking at *get over sb/sth* on p. 104.

BUILD YOUR VOCABULARY

SIMILAR VERBS

The verb **get over** describes an action. To describe a state, use **be over**:
*He had a nasty bout of flu, but he's **over** it now.*

TURN OVER; TURN *somebody or something* OVER

STUDY Read these sentences carefully.

- He **turned over** and went back to sleep.
- The car skidded on the ice and **turned over**.
- She **turned** the book **over** and read the notes on the back cover.
- This animal uses its nose to **turn over** stones when it is looking for food.
- Cook the steak for a few minutes, then **turn** it **over** to cook the other side.
- Can you match one of your cards to the one that has **been turned over**?

CHECK Use the sentences in the Study box to help you do these exercises.

MEANING

Turn over; turn somebody or something over means 'to change your position or the position of somebody or something'. How? Choose <u>one</u> answer.

a) so that the other side is facing outwards or upwards
b) so that the top is facing downwards
c) so that the inside is facing outwards

GRAMMAR

Which of the following are grammatically possible?

a) He turned over.
b) He turned the book over.
c) He turned over the book.
d) He turned it over.
e) He turned over it.
f) The book was turned over.

Now check your answers by looking at *turn over; turn sb/sth over* on p. 110.

PRACTISE

1 What does *it* refer to in each sentence? Use each object below once only.

a question paper   a postcard   a card   a hand

a) Take one from anywhere in the pack and turn it over.
b) Despite all the revision, his mind went blank as soon as he turned it over.
c) He turned it over and looked at the lines on her palm.
d) She looked at the picture, then turned it over to see the postmark.

2 Complete the following sentences in an appropriate way, using *turn over* and an object (a noun or a pronoun) <u>if necessary</u>:

a) He ...., trying to find a more comfortable position.
b) She picked up the coin and examined it carefully, ... in her hands.
c) Shall I .... and cook the other side now?

Now check your answers by looking at *turn over; turn sb/sth over* on p. 109.

COME ROUND

STUDY Read these sentences carefully.

- Jill **came round** last night and stayed for hours.
- Would you like to **come round** for dinner?
- I'll **come round** to your hotel as soon as I finish work.
- **Come round** later and we'll show you our wedding photos.

CHECK Use the sentences in the Study box to help you do these exercises.

MEANING

If you ask somebody to *come round*, are you asking them to:
a) stay with you for a few days?
b) visit you at your home for a short time?
c) meet you somewhere?

GRAMMAR

Which of these are grammatically possible?
a) He came round.
b) He came round my house.
c) He came round to my house.
d) My house was come round to.

Now check your answers by looking at *come round* on p. 102.

PRACTISE

1 Complete the following in an appropriate way, using a form of *come round* in each:
a) My parents usually .... our place on Sundays.
b) If you're free on Friday evening, do .... coffee.
c) My phone's broken. Can .... use yours?
d) I'm busy tomorrow evening. Some friends ....

2 Invite your friend to your house for lunch on Saturday:

....

Now check your answers by looking at *come round* on p. 102.

BUILD YOUR VOCABULARY

SIMILAR VERBS

You can use **come around**, especially in American English, or **come over**, instead of **come round**:

*Our new neighbours are **coming over** for a drink later.*
*He doesn't **come around** much any more. He's very busy with his new job.*

Use **go round** or **go over** instead of **come round** or **come over** when you are talking about somebody else's home:
*Why don't you **go round** to your grandmother's today?*
*I'm **going over** to see Anne later.*

BE UP TO *somebody*

STUDY Read these sentences carefully.

- It **was up to** Roger to make sure all the doors and windows were locked.
- The decision**'s** not **up to** her, it**'s up to** her manager.
- It's your birthday, so what we do tonight **is up to** you.
- 'Can I have a computer for Christmas?' 'That**'s up to** your father.'

CHECK Use the sentences in the Study box to help you do these exercises.

MEANING
The verb *be up to somebody* has two related meanings. What does it
mean in the following examples? Choose a) or b) in each case.

1 **It was up to her to cook dinner on Mondays.**
   a) It was her decision.
   b) It was her responsibility.

2 **'Shall we go out?' 'It's up to you.'**
   a) It is your decision.
   b) It is your responsibility.

GRAMMAR
Which of these are grammatically possible?
   a) It's the boss up to.
   b) It's up to the boss.
   c) It's her up to.
   d) It's up to her.

   Now check your answers by looking at *be up to sb* on p. 101.

PRACTISE

1 **Complete the following with the correct form of *be up to somebody*
   and one of the objects below:**

   you   students   her   the prosecution lawyer
   a) It .... to find their own accommodation.
   b) It .... to prove that somebody is guilty in court.
   c) I don't mind where we go - it ....
   d) Jenny can go to the party if she likes - it ....

2 **Answer the following questions in an appropriate way, using *be up to
   somebody* in each answer:**
   a) Can you have time off work next week?
      That's up to ....
   b) Does your mother tidy your room for you?
      No, it's ....
   c) Will he go to jail?
      That's ....
   Now check your answers by looking at *be up to sb* on p. 101.

BE UP TO *something*

STUDY Read these sentences carefully.

- He looks very guilty. What do you think he**'s been up to**?
- The kids are very quiet. **Are** they **up to** something?
- She didn't really want to know what he**'d been up to**.

CHECK Use the sentences in the Study box to help you do these exercises.

MEANING

1 Which of the choices a) - d) mean the same as the sentence below?

   What are you up to?

   a) What is your job?
   b) What are you doing?
   c) Where are you?
   d) What do you think?

**2 If you *are up to something*, is it usually
something <u>good</u>, something <u>bad</u> or
something <u>important</u>?**

GRAMMAR

Which of these are grammatically possible?
   a) He's up to something.
   b) He's something up to.
   c) Something was up to him.

   Now check your answers by looking at *be up to sth* on p. 101.

PRACTISE

1 Match the two halves to make complete sentences:
   a) I'm going to tell his parents   **i)** What have you been up to?
   b) We have to find out   **ii)** what he's been up to.
   c) I haven't seen you for weeks.   **iii)** what these people are up to.
   d) He's gone out again.   **iv)** I think he's up to something.

**2 Write an appropriate question for each of the following, including *be
up to* in each:**
   a) Your friend is very tired this morning. Ask what he/she did last night.
      So, ...?
   b) A little boy is covered in mud. Ask his mother what he has been doing.
      ....?
   c) The children are very quiet. Ask your friend if he/she thinks they are doing
      something naughty.
      Do you think ....?

   Now check your answers by looking at *be up to sth* on p. 101.

BLOW UP; BLOW *somebody or something* UP

STUDY **Read these sentences carefully.**

- There was a huge bang as the fuel tank **blew up**.
- In 1605 Guy Fawkes tried to **blow up** Parliament and the King.
- They threatened to **blow** the building **up**.
- The thieves robbed the store and then **blew** it **up**.
- The two men **were** tragically **blown up** by a car bomb in 1987.

CHECK **Use the sentences in the Study box to help you do these exercises.**

MEANING

I If something *blows up*, what happens? Choose the best meaning:
   a) it explodes or is destroyed by an explosion
   b) it is badly damaged or destroyed by a strong wind

2 If somebody or something *blows something up*, what happens?
   a) it is destroyed with a bomb or an explosion
   b) it is knocked to the ground and badly damaged by strong winds

GRAMMAR

Which of these are grammatically possible?
   a) The factory blew up.
   b) They blew the factory up.
   c) They blew up the factory.
   d) They blew it up.
   e) They blew up it.
   f) The factory was blown up.

Now check your answers by looking at *blow up; blow sb/sth up* on p. 101.

PRACTISE

Complete the following with the correct form of *blow up, blow somebody or something up* and one of the objects below <u>where necessary</u>:

the offices   the company director   it

a) The demonstrators threatened to .... if their demands were not met.
b) We were sent home from school when the old heating boiler ....
c) They laid explosives all along the bridge and ....
d) An attempt was made to ...., but luckily he escaped unharmed.

Now check your answers by looking at *blow up; blow sb/sth up* on p. 101.

BUILD YOUR VOCABULARY

RELATED WORDS

noun: **blow-up** (= an explosion) *(This is especially used in American English.)*
The mixture of chemicals caused a massive **blow-up**.

BLOW *something* UP

STUDY Read these sentences carefully.

- We **blew up** lots of balloons for the party.
- They used the pump to **blow** the air bed **up**.
- The balloon will burst if you **blow** it **up** too much.
- Can you check the tyres? I think they need to **be blown up** a bit.

CHECK Use the sentences in the Study box to help you do these exercises.

MEANING

1 Use two of these words to complete this meaning of *blow something up*:

water   gas   air   petrol   wind

to fill something with .... or ....

2 Which of the following can you *blow up*?
 a) a ball   **b)** a balloon   **c)** your cheeks   **d)** a tyre   **e)** a car

GRAMMAR

Which of these are grammatically possible?
a) We blew the balloons up.
b) We blew up the balloons.
c) We blew them up.
d) We blew up them.
e) The balloons were blown up.

> **Now check your answers by looking at *blow sth up* on p. 101.**

PRACTISE

Answer these questions in any way you like, using the verb *blow something up* in each:
a) Is everything ready for the party?
     No, ...
b) Did you check the tyres on my bicycle for me?

   ....

> **Now check your answers by looking at *blow sth up* on p. 101.**

BUILD YOUR VOCABULARY

RELATED WORDS
adjective: **blow-up** *(This is only used before a noun.)*
We bought him a **blow-up** *pillow for the long bus journey.*

OTHER MEANINGS
Blow something up also means 'to make something larger', for example a photograph, a picture, etc:
What a lovely photo! Shall we have it **blown up***?*

BREAK UP

Read these sentences carefully.

- It's always hard when a marriage **breaks up**, especially if there are children.
- After three albums, the band **broke up** in order to have solo careers.
- He's just **broken up** with his girlfriend.
- 'Why are you crying?' 'Chris thinks we should **break up**.'

CHECK **Use the sentences in the Study box to help you do these exercises.**

MEANING
Complete the meanings with a word or phrase from the brackets:
a) If a relationship breaks up, it .... *(is unhappy / comes to an end)*
b) If people break up, they .... *(end a relationship / get divorced)*

GRAMMAR
Which of these are grammatically possible?
a) They broke up.
b) He broke up.
c) He broke up with her.
d) The marriage broke up.

Now check your answers by looking at *break up* on p. 101.

PRACTISE

1 **Complete the sentences with one of the subjects below, using each subject only once:**

her marriage   many bands   she

a) .... broke up in 1985, leaving her to raise two children on her own.

b) .... break up because of personality clashes between members.

c) Pat was very depressed after .... broke up with John.

2 **Answer the following question in two ways, using *break up*:**
   Are Mark and Liz still together?
      No, ...
      Yes, ...

Now check your answers by looking at *break up* on p. 101.

BUILD YOUR VOCABULARY

RELATED WORDS
noun: **break-up** *(This noun is usually countable.)*
*He moved away after the **break-up** of his marriage.*

SYNONYMS
Split up means the same as **break up** and is used in the same way:
*Did you know Sue has **split up** with Jake?*

BRING *somebody* UP

STUDY Read these sentences carefully.

- I would prefer not to **bring** my children **up** in a big city.
- My aunt **brought up** her three children without any help.
- His mother **brought** him **up** to always say 'please' and 'thank you'.
- She **was brought up** in the countryside.

CHECK Use the sentences in the Study box to help you do these exercises.

MEANING
If you *bring up* a child, what do you do? Choose <u>two</u> answers:
a) you care for him or her until he or she is an adult
b) you make him or her behave in an adult way
c) you teach him or her how to behave

GRAMMAR
Which of these are grammatically possible?
a) She brought her son up.
b) She brought up her son.
c) She brought him up.
d) She brought up him.
e) He was brought up.

Now check your answers by looking at *bring sb up* on p. 101.

PRACTISE

1 Complete each of these sentences with the correct form of *bring up* and one of the words or phrases below:

I   him   boys and girls

a) His parents died when he was young, so his grandparents ....
b) Do you think parents should .... in the same way?
c) .... on a farm.

2 Now use *bring somebody up* to write two sentences about <u>your</u> childhood.

....

....

Now check your answers by looking at *bring sb up* on p. 101.

BUILD YOUR VOCABULARY

RELATED WORDS
noun: **upbringing** (= the way in which a child is cared for and taught, especially by parents, while he or she is growing up) *(This noun can be either singular or uncountable.)*
*She had a very strict **upbringing**.*

SIMILAR VERBS
➤ *grow up* and *look after somebody*

CATCH UP; CATCH *somebody or something* UP

Read these sentences carefully.

- They're a long way in front. Do you think we can **catch up**?
- He ran to **catch up** with her.
- You go ahead. I'll **catch** you **up** in a few minutes.
- The police finally **caught up** with the car at the traffic lights.

CHECK **Use the sentences in the Study box to help you do these exercises.**

MEANING
Imagine you are running a race. If you *catch up* with somebody, which of these statements are true?
a) They were ahead of you.
b) You had to run faster than them.
c) They are still in front of you.
d) You arc now in front of them.
e) You are now level with them.

GRAMMAR
Which of these are grammatically possible?
a) She caught up.
b) She caught Tom up.
c) She caught up Tom.
d) She caught him up.
e) She caught up with Tom.

Now check your answers by looking at *catch up; catch sb/sth up* on p. 101.

PRACTISE

Complete these sentences, using a form of *catch up* or *catch somebody or something up* and any other necessary information:
a) He told me to go on ahead and said he ....
b) She was driving so fast that I ....
c) I often had to stop and let him ....
d) If you run fast nobody ....

Now check your answers by looking at *catch up; catch sb/sth up* on p. 101.

BUILD YOUR VOCABULARY

OTHER MEANINGS
This verb can also be used to mean 'to reach the same level or standard as somebody or something else that was better or more advanced':
*She missed some classes and had to work hard to **catch up** with the rest of the class.*
*The company will probably **catch up** with its competitors within a couple of years.*

SIMILAR VERBS
Also look at the verb **keep up**, which has a similar meaning.

CHEER UP; CHEER *somebody or yourself* UP

STUDY **Read these sentences carefully.**

- **Cheer up**! I'm sure everything will be fine.
- He **cheered up** a lot when he saw you.
- He spent ages trying to **cheer** the kids **up**.
- How can I **cheer** you **up**?
- I went shopping to **cheer** myself **up**.
- Maria **was cheered up** by a letter from her mother.

CHECK **Use the sentences in the Study box to help you do these exercises.**

MEANING
If you *cheer up*, how do you feel?
a) happier than before
b) healthier than before
c) more excited than before

GRAMMAR
Which of these are grammatically possible?
a) She cheered up.
b) She cheered herself up.
c) She cheered up herself.
d) She cheered her friend up.
e) She cheered him up.
f) She was cheered up.

**Now check your answers by looking at *cheer up; cheer sb/yourself up*
on p. 102.**

PRACTISE

I What could you say in response to the following? Use *cheer up* or *cheer somebody up* in each answer.
a) I'm worried about Jo. She seems very depressed.
   Why don't you ....?
b) Is Chris more cheerful now?
   Yes. He ....
c) I'm tired of this cold winter weather.
   ....

2 When you are feeling depressed, what do you do to *cheer yourself up*? Write a full sentence.
   ....

**Now check your answers by looking at *cheer up; cheer sb/yourself up*
on p. 102.**

DO *something* UP

STUDY Read these sentences carefully.

- I've eaten so much that I can't **do** my trousers **up**!
- He couldn't **do up** the buttons on his coat.
- The skirt was far too small for her - she couldn't even **do** it **up**.
- He wore a long coat that **was done up** at the neck.

CHECK Use the sentences in the Study box to help you do these exercises.

MEANING

1 Choose the best explanation of this meaning of *do something up*:
   a) to make something tight
   b) to fasten or close something

2 Which of these can you *do up*?
   a) a jacket   **b)** fingers   **c)** a zip   **d)** socks   **e)** a button

GRAMMAR

Which of these are grammatically possible?
a) He did his coat up.
b) He did up his coat.
c) He did it up.
d) He did up it.
e) His coat was done up.

Now check your answers by looking at *do sth up* on p. 103.

PRACTISE

Respond to the following, using a form of *do something up* in each:
a) Do you think this jacket is smart enough?

   Yes, if you ....
b) Why didn't you buy those jeans?

   They were too small. ....!
c) I just tripped and fell.

   I'm not surprised. Your laces ....

Now check your answers by looking at *do sth up* on p. 103.

BUILD YOUR VOCABULARY

OPPOSITES

The opposite of **do something up** is **undo something**:
*I can't **undo** my zip. I think it's stuck.*

SIMILAR VERBS

You can also use more specific verbs: **button up**, **zip up** and **tie up**:
*She helped him **button up** his coat.*
The opposites of these verbs are **unbutton**, **unzip** and **untie**.

FILL *something* UP

STUDY Read these sentences carefully.

- He **filled** Daisy's glass **up** again.
- My mother **filled up** the freezer for me before she went away.
- I keep emptying the box, but you keep **filling** it **up** again!
- We were so thirsty the water jug had to **be filled up** three times.

CHECK Use the sentences in the Study box to help you do these exercises.

MEANING

If you *fill up* a container or a place, it becomes completely full. Which of these can you *fill up*?

a) a glass   **b)** a jug   **c)** a sandwich   **d)** a suitcase   **e)** a job

f) an order   **g)** a jacket

GRAMMAR

Which of the following are grammatically possible?

a) He filled the bottle up.
b) He filled up the bottle.
c) He filled it up.
d) He filled up it.
e) The bottle was filled up.

Now check your answers by looking at *fill sth up* on p. 103.

PRACTISE

Complete these sentences in any way you like, using the verb *fill up* and an object (a noun or a pronoun):

a) She emptied her glass and .... again.
b) If you want some more water, ... from the tap.
c) The fridge is almost empty! I only .... last week!
d) You don't need to .... just to make one cup of tea!

Now check your answers by looking at *fill sth up* on p. 103.

BUILD YOUR VOCABULARY

OTHER MEANINGS

Fill something up is very often used to talk about putting petrol in a car:
*We must **fill** the car **up** with petrol before we go.*
*Take the car to the garage and **fill** it **up**.*
You can also use **fill up** with this meaning:
*Don't forget to **fill up** before we go. It's a long journey.*
*I used the car for a week and then **filled up** (with petrol).*

GET UP; GET *somebody* UP

> **STUDY** Read these sentences carefully.
>
> • What time do you have to **get up** tomorrow?
> • Hurry up! It's time to **get up**!
> • It's 8.30 and Mark's still in bed. I'd better go and **get** him **up**.

CHECK Use the sentences in the Study box to help you do these exercises.

MEANING
What is the <u>opposite</u> of *get up*? Choose <u>one</u> answer.
a) stop sleeping   **b)** go to bed   **c)** get out of bed

GRAMMAR
Which of these are grammatically possible?
a) She got up.
b) She got her son up.
c) She got up her son.
d) She got him up.
e) She got up him.
f) He was got up.

Now check your answers by looking at *get up; get sb up* on p. 104.

PRACTISE

1 Answer these questions about <u>yourself</u>, using *get up* in each case.
   a) What time do you usually get up during the week?

   ....

   b) What about at the weekend?

   ....

   c) And this morning?

   ....

   d) What about tomorrow?

   ....

**2 It is nearly midday and your teenage son is still in bed. What do you
   say to him?**
   ....!

   Now check your answers by looking at *get up; get sb up* on p. 104.

BUILD YOUR VOCABULARY

SIMILAR VERBS
Get up is an action. The verb **be up** describes a state:
*He **was up** (= he was out of bed) and dressed by six o'clock.*
➤ *wake up; wake somebody up*

GIVE UP; GIVE UP *something*

FIRST MEANING

STUDY Read these sentences carefully.

- I **give up** - tell me the answer.
- I tried running, but I **gave up** after about ten minutes.
- Nick tried to fix the car, but **gave up** the attempt after an hour.
- It was so difficult that she was tempted to **give** it all **up**.
- In the end he **gave up** trying to explain it all to me.

CHECK Use the sentences in the Study box to help you do these exercises.

MEANING

Use the words below to complete this meaning of *give up, give up something*:

difficult   stop   trying   usually

to .... to do something, ... because it is too

....

GRAMMAR

Which of these are grammatically possible?

a) He gave up.
b) He gave up the attempt.
c) He gave it up.
d) He gave up it.
e) He gave up to try.
f) He gave up trying.

Now check your answers by looking at *give up; give up sth* on p. 104.

PRACTISE

1 Match the two halves to make complete sentences:

a) They gave up the search	**i)** until the solution is found.
b) We will not give up	**ii)** when it got dark.
c) I was tempted to give it up	**iii)** unless you're sure you won't succeed.
d) Don't give up trying	**iv)** and go home.

2 Rewrite the following so that the meaning stays the same, using a form of *give up, give up something*:

a) Don't stop trying - I know you can do it!

   Don't ....*!*

b) I couldn't find him, and in the end I abandoned the search.

   ....

c) He was exhausted, but he was determined to continue.

   ....

Now check your answers by looking at *give up; give up sth* on p. 104.

GIVE UP; GIVE UP *something*

SECOND MEANING

STUDY Read these sentences carefully.

- Do you still smoke? You really should **give up**, you know.
- Try **giving up** all animal milks and drinking soya milk instead.
- No chocolate for me, thanks. I've **given** it **up**.
- I **gave up** drinking coffee because it kept me awake at night.

CHECK Use the sentences in the Study box to help you do these exercises.

MEANING

If you *give up something*, you stop doing or having something. Why?
a) because it is too difficult
b) because you consider it unhealthy
c) because you are not allowed to do or have it

GRAMMAR

Which of these are grammatically possible?
a) She gave up.
b) She gave up coffee.
c) She gave it up.
d) She gave up it.
e) She gave up to drink coffee.
f) She gave up drinking coffee.

Now check your answers by looking at *give up; give up sth* on p. 104.

PRACTISE

1 Respond to the following, using a form of *give up* in each response and any other necessary information:
a) Do you still smoke?
  Yes, I'm afraid so. I ....
b) Would you like a coffee?
  No thanks. ....

2 Are <u>you</u> trying to *give anything up*, or have you recently *given something up*? Is there anything that you think you should *give up*?

....

....

Now check your answers by looking at *give up; give up sth* on p. 104.

BUILD YOUR VOCABULARY

OPPOSITES
➤ **take up something**

SIMILAR VERBS
Also look at the verb **cut down**, which has a related meaning.

GROW UP

STUDY Read these sentences carefully.

- They moved around a lot while the children were **growing up**.
- He wants to be a firefighter when he **grows up**.
- I **grew up** in a big city.
- Oh, **grow up**! Stop being so childish!

CHECK Use the sentences in the Study box to help you do these exercises.

MEANING

Which one of the following does <u>not</u> explain the meaning of *grow up*?

a) to increase in size, number, etc.

b) to spend the time when you are a child in a particular place or manner

c) to become an adult

GRAMMAR

Which of these are grammatically possible?

a) Grow up!

b) Grow yourself up!

c) She grew up.

d) She grew up her daughter.

Now check your answers by looking at *grow up* on p. 105.

PRACTISE

1 *Grow* **or** *grow up*? **Remember that** *grow* **means 'become bigger or taller'. Choose the best alternative:**

a) Hasn't he *grown/grown up*! He's nearly as tall as his father now!

b) That plant has really *grown/grown up* since the last time I saw it.

c) Thomas and I *grew/grew up* together, so we're very close.

2 Answer these questions about <u>yourself</u>, using the verb *grow up*:

a) When you were a child, where did you live?

....

b) What did you want to be when you were an adult?

....

Now check your answers by looking at *grow up* on p. 105.

BUILD YOUR VOCABULARY

RELATED WORDS

adjective: **grown-up**

They have three children, all of them **grown-up** *now.*

noun: **a grown-up** *(This is used by children, or by adults talking to children.)*

Do you want to come over here and sit with the **grown-ups**?

SIMILAR VERBS

➤ *bring somebody up*

84

HANG UP; HANG UP *something*

STUDY Read these sentences carefully.

- I said goodbye and **hung up**.
- The number you dialled is busy. Please **hang up** and try again.
- As soon as he **hung up** the phone, it rang again.
- Don't **hang up** on me, please. We need to talk.

CHECK Use the sentences in the Study box to help you do these exercises.

MEANING

1 Why do you *hang up*?
  a) to start a telephone conversation
  b) to continue a telephone conversation
  c) to end a telephone conversation

2 If you *hang up on somebody*, what do you do?
  a) you suddenly answer the phone for somebody
  b) you suddenly put down the receiver in the middle of a conversation
  c) you suddenly stop speaking to somebody on the telephone and wait

GRAMMAR
Which of these are grammatically possible?
  a) I hung up.
  b) I hung the phone up.
  c) I hung up the phone.
  d) I hung up him.
  e) I hung up on him.

Now check your answers by looking at *hang up; hang up sth* on p. 105.

PRACTISE

Complete the sentences with the correct form of *hang up* and one of
the phrases below:

immediately   on me   the phone   when we've finished
  a) Do you want to speak to Mum, or shall I ....?
  b) When I answered the phone, the caller ....
  c) 'What did he say?' 'Nothing. He ....!'
  d) 'Sorry, wrong number,' she said, ...

Now check your answers by looking at *hang up; hang up sth* on p. 105.

BUILD YOUR VOCABULARY

OTHER MEANINGS
Hang something up also means 'to hang something on a hook, a piece of string, etc.':
*Shall I **hang** your coat **up** for you, sir?*
*The wedding dress **was hung up** in the closet.*

HOLD *somebody or something* UP

STUDY Read these sentences carefully.

- Roadworks on the motorway are **holding up** the traffic again.
- Opposition to the road and a lack of cash have **held up** progress.
- I'm sorry to be so slow. Am I **holding** people **up**?
- Isn't Rose here yet? I'll go and see what's **holding** her **up**.
- John's not home yet. He must have **been held up** at the office.

CHECK Use the sentences in the Study box to help you do these exercises.

MEANING
Choose <u>two</u> of the verbs below to complete the meaning of *hold somebody or something up*:

block   cancel   control   delay

to .... or .... the progress of somebody or something

GRAMMAR
Which of these are grammatically possible?
a) She held the meeting up.
b) She held up the meeting.
c) She held it up.
d) She held up it.
e) The meeting was held up.

Now check your answers by looking at *hold sb/sth up* on p. 105.

PRACTISE

1 **Complete these sentences using one of the words or phrases below and a <u>passive</u> form of *hold somebody or something up*:**

he   the boat   traffic   they

a) I'm sorry my father is not here. .... in Chicago on business.
b) Sue and the kids are late. .... in traffic.
c) They had enough food for several days in case .... by gales.
d) Several roads were blocked, and .... for over an hour.

2 **Correct any errors in the following:**
a) I holded things up for an hour while I rearranged the furniture.
b) She held everybody up by arguing with the waiter about the bill.
c) Every time there's bad weather, the trains are being held up.

Now check your answers by looking at *hold sb/sth up* on p. 105.

BUILD YOUR VOCABULARY

RELATED WORDS
noun: **a hold-up**
*Why has the train stopped? What's the **hold-up**?*

KEEP UP

STUDY Read these sentences carefully.

- He was walking very fast and I almost had to run to **keep up**.
- Slow down! I can't **keep up**.
- The car behind went through a red light to **keep up** with us.
- Jack was walking fast, but I **kept up** with him.

CHECK Use the sentences in the Study box to help you do these exercises.

MEANING

Which one of the following is the best explanation of this meaning of *keep up* ?
a) to move at the same rate or speed as somebody or something
b) to move more slowly than somebody or something
c) to move faster than somebody or something

GRAMMAR

Which of the following are grammatically possible?
a) I couldn't keep up.
b) I couldn't keep up him.
c) I couldn't keep up with him.
d) He couldn't be kept up with.

Now check your answers by looking at *keep up* on p. 105.

PRACTISE

1 Complete these sentences in a suitable way, using the verb *keep up*:
a) Hurry up! Please try ....!
b) You're walking too fast! ....!
c) We forgot that little Joe would have difficulty ....

2 *Keep up* or *catch up*? Look at the answer to the **MEANING** exercise and at the verb *catch up* on p. 77 and then choose the best verb:
a) He's too far ahead now. You'll never *catch up/keep up* with him.
b) Let's wait here until the others *catch up/keep up*.
c) We walked along together, Jim almost running to *catch up/keep up* with me.

Now check your answers by looking at *keep up* on p. 105.

BUILD YOUR VOCABULARY

OTHER MEANINGS

This verb is often used to mean **1** 'to progress or increase at the same speed as somebody or something else': *Wages are not **keeping up** with inflation.*
*He didn't like maths and was struggling to **keep up** with the rest of the class.*
2 'to deal successfully with a situation that changes rapidly':
*The company is finding it hard to **keep up** with demand.*

SIMILAR VERBS

➤ *catch up; catch somebody or something up*

LOOK *something* UP

STUDY Read these sentences carefully.

- Joe's **looking up** their number in the phone book.
- I had to **look** several words **up** in the dictionary.
- I don't know when the course starts, but I'll **look** it **up** for you.
- He didn't know my phone number, but he **looked** me **up** in the book.

CHECK Use the sentences in the Study box to help you do these exercises.

MEANING
Complete the meaning of *look something up* with a word or phrase from the brackets:

to *(guess / search for)* a word or some *(information / names)* in a *(book / dictionary)* or on a computer

GRAMMAR
Which of these are grammatically possible?
a) He looked the word up.
b) He looked up the word.
c) He looked it up.
d) He looked up it.
e) He looked him up.

> Now check your answers by looking at *look sth up* on p. 106.

PRACTISE

1 There is a grammatical mistake in <u>one</u> of these sentences. Can you find the mistake and correct it?
a) I enjoy using a dictionary and looking up new words.
b) I usually look up new words up in a bilingual dictionary.
c) I only use the Internet as a resource, for looking up useful information.
d) I don't know where Brunei is - I would have to look it up on a map.

2 Complete the following sentences with the correct form of *look something up* and one of the objects below:

her number   something   it

a) Every time I try to ...., the Internet crashes.
b) Why don't you .... in the phone book if you want to talk to her?
c) The next train leaves at six o'clock. I .... on the timetable.

> Now check your answers by looking at *look sth up* on p. 106.

BUILD YOUR VOCABULARY

RELATED WORDS
noun: **look-up** *(This noun can be countable and uncountable.)*
*The new software has an instant **look-up** facility, which is useful for reading web pages.*

MAKE *something* UP

STUDY Read these sentences carefully.

- I don't believe you! You've **made up** the whole story.
- She loves singing and even **makes up** her own songs.
- He didn't know the true facts so he **made** them **up**.
- The figures are not real but have **been made up** as an example.

CHECK Use the sentences in the Study box to help you do these exercises.

MEANING

Which of the following is closest in meaning to *make something up*?
- **a)** to emphasize something
- **b)** to imagine something
- **c)** to invent something

GRAMMAR

Which of these are grammatically correct?
- **a)** He made up an excuse.
- **b)** He made it up.
- **c)** He made up it.
- **d)** It was made up.

Now check your answers by looking at *make sth up* **on p. 106.**

PRACTISE

1 Answer the following questions in an appropriate way, using *make up* **and a suitable object (a noun or a pronoun):**
- **a)** Do you believe him?
   No, I think he ....
- **b)** Is this a true story?
   No, it ....
- **c)** What excuse did you give for being late?
   Oh, I ....
- **d)** I don't think you're telling the truth.
   I promise I ....

2 Correct any errors in these sentences:
- **a)** Of course it's not true! I made it all up!
- **b)** Most of what had been written about her in the papers had made up.
- **c)** He can't have make up all that stuff about the army, can he?

Now check your answers by looking at *make sth up* **on p. 106.**

BUILD YOUR VOCABULARY

RELATED WORDS

adjective: **made-up** (= invented; not true or real)
*It was a true story, not a **made-up** one.*

OWN UP; OWN UP TO *something*

- Are you sure he did it? Did he **own up**?
- Don't be afraid to **own up to** your mistakes.
- A vase had been broken, but nobody **owned up to** it.
- Will anybody **own up to** breaking the window?

CHECK Use the sentences in the Study box to help you do these exercises.

MEANING

Choose the best meaning of *own up; own up to something*:

a) to admit that you are responsible for something that has happened
b) to say that something belongs to you
c) to feel guilty about something that has happened

GRAMMAR

Which of the following are grammatically possible?

a) She owned up.
b) She owned up her mistake.
c) She owned up to her mistake.
d) She owned up to it.
e) She owned up to make a mistake.
f) She owned up to making a mistake.
g) The mistake was owned up to.

Now check your answers by looking at *own up; own up to sth* on p. 107.

PRACTISE

1 If you *own up to something,* which of the following might you say?

a) It was my idea!
b) It was him!
c) It wasn't me!
d) I did it!
e) I don't know who did it!

2 Complete these sentences with the correct form of *own up* or *own up to:*

a) Eventually the boys .... inventing the story as a joke.
b) When none of the staff ...., they all lost their jobs.
c) If the person responsible ...., they won't be punished.
d) In the end I felt so guilty that I couldn't help ....
e) She was close to tears as she .... taking the money.
f) For some reason he refuses to .... his mistakes.

Now check your answers by looking at *own up; own up to sth* on p. 107.

PICK *somebody or something* **UP**

FIRST MEANING

STUDY **Read these sentences carefully.**

- He **picked up** my bags and took them to my room.
- **Pick** your books **up** off the floor, please.
- If the baby starts crying, **pick** him **up**.
- Mary was crying to **be picked up** and carried.

CHECK **Use the sentences in the Study box to help you do these exercises.**

MEANING
Which of the following means almost the same as *pick somebody or something up*?

a) to carry **b)** to choose **c)** to lift **d)** to hold

GRAMMAR
Which of the following are grammatically possible?

a) I picked the pen up.
b) I picked up the pen.
c) I picked it up.
d) I picked up it.
e) The pen was picked up.

Now check your answers by looking at *pick sb/sth up* on p. 107.

PRACTISE

Complete the following with the correct form of *pick up* and one of the objects below:

her clothes   her   it   my credit card   a card

a) He dropped his hat, so I .... for him.
b) When it's your turn, you have to .... from the pile.
c) She was so heavy that I could only just ....
d) I spent a few minutes .... off the floor and hanging them in the closet.
e) Did you .... by mistake? I think I left it on the table.

Now check your answers by looking at *pick sb/sth up* on p. 107.

BUILD YOUR VOCABULARY

IDIOMS
pick up the pieces
This idiom means 'to return, or to help somebody return, to a normal situation, particularly after a shock or disaster':
*He walked out on his family, leaving his wife to **pick up the pieces**.*

OPPOSITES
➤ *put somebody or something down*

PICK *somebody or something* UP

SECOND MEANING

- I have to **pick** the kids **up** from school this afternoon.
- We can **pick up** the tickets an hour before the show starts.
- Shall I **pick** you **up** from work today?
- What time are you **being picked up** in the morning?

CHECK Use the sentences in the Study box to help you do these exercises.

MEANING

1 If you *pick somebody up*, what do you do? Choose the best meaning:
  a) you help somebody to go somewhere
  b) you collect them in your vehicle and take them somewhere

2 Choose the verb that means almost the same as *pick something up*:
  a) to collect something   b) to find something   c) to choose something

GRAMMAR

Which of these are grammatically possible?
  a) He picked the tickets up.
  b) He picked up the tickets.
  c) He picked them up.
  d) He picked up them.
  e) The tickets were picked up.

  Now check your answers by looking at *pick sb/sth up* on p. 107.

PRACTISE

Complete these sentences using a form of the verb *pick up*, the phrase in brackets and an appropriate object (a noun or a pronoun):
  a) I can't meet you at 3.30. I have to .... *(from school)*
  b) We need to .... *(from the Box Office)*
  c) I'm working late tonight. I can't .... *(until eight)*
  d) He had to go home first and .... *(for the weekend)*
  Now check your answers by looking at *pick sb/sth up* on p. 107.

BUILD YOUR VOCABULARY

RELATED WORDS

noun: **a pickup** (= an occasion when somebody or something is collected)
The bus driver made several **pickups** *before heading for the airport.*

OPPOSITES

➤ *drop somebody or something off*

OTHER MEANINGS

Pick somebody up also means 'to stop and let somebody get in your vehicle':
I was warned never to **pick up** *hitchhikers when I was driving on my own.*

PUT UP WITH *somebody or something*

STUDY Read these sentences carefully.

- She **put up with** her noisy neighbours for years.
- I find him very annoying. I don't know how she **puts up with** him.
- I am not **putting up with** that sort of behaviour!
- He says it's a nuisance but he can **put up with** it.
- I hate the city, but we **put up with** living there because of our jobs.

CHECK Use the sentences in the Study box to help you do these exercises.

MEANING
Which of the following means the same as *put up with*?

a) to continue   **b)** to tolerate   **c)** to be annoyed

GRAMMAR
Which of these are grammatically possible?

a) She put up with the noise.
b) She put it up with.
c) She put up with it.
d) She put up with live there.
e) She put up with living there.
f) The noise was put up with.

Now check your answers by looking at *put up with sb/sth* **on p. 108.**

PRACTISE

1 What is *it* in each sentence? Match each with one of the words below.

the noise   this behaviour   the dust   the weather   the problem

a) It's a bit cold, but I can put up with it.
b) I won't put up with it. I'm going to tell them to keep quiet.
c) It can't be fixed until Friday, so we'll just have to put up with it.
d) I've tried to put up with it but it makes me sneeze.
e) Why is she doing this? I'm not going to put up with it!

2 Answer the following questions using the verb *put up with*. The first one has been done for you as an example.

a) Why did you decide to leave your job?
Because I couldn't put up with my boss any longer.
b) Why don't you like him?
Because ....
c) Why did you leave your job in the city?
Because ....
d) Do you like living in the country, then?
No, but ....

Now check your answers by looking at *put up with sb/sth* **on p. 108.**

SET *something* UP

STUDY Read these sentences carefully.

- They often talked about **setting up** their own business.
- He **set** the company **up** three and a half years ago.
- The company is still run by Anna Marsh, who **set** it **up** in 1983.
- She **set up** a group for single parents and their children.
- A committee **was set up** to investigate the problems.

CHECK Use the sentences in the Study box to help you do these exercises.

MEANING

If you *set something up*, what do you do?

a) you control something
b) you create or start something
c) you arrange or manage something

GRAMMAR

Which of these are grammatically possible?

a) He set the system up.
b) He set up the system.
c) He set it up.
d) He set up it.
e) The system was set up.

Now check your answers by looking at *set sth up* on p. 108.

PRACTISE

1 **Write the questions to fit these answers, using *set something up* correctly in each. Try to use a variety of structures.**

a) What kind of company did he set up?

It manufactures computer software.

b) ....?

In 1992.

c) ....?

Because he was tired of working for other people.

d) ....?

I don't think so. One is enough!

2 **Would you like to set up your own business? Write a full sentence below, giving the reason(s) for your answer.**

....

Now check your answers by looking at *set sth up* on p. 108.

SPEAK UP

STUDY Read these sentences carefully.

- You'll have to **speak up**, I'm afraid. Mrs. Newton is rather deaf.
- **Speak up**! I can't hear a word you're saying!
- Can you **speak up** a bit? People at the back of the room can't hear you.

CHECK Use the sentences in the Study box to help you do these exercises.

MEANING
If you ask somebody to *speak up*, what do you want them to do?
Choose <u>one</u> answer.
a) shout
b) speak faster
c) speak louder
d) repeat something because you didn't understand it

GRAMMAR
Which of these are grammatically possible?
a) Speak up.
b) She spoke up.
c) She was spoken up.

Now check your answers by looking at *speak up* on p. 108.

PRACTISE

1 **In which of these situations might you ask somebody to *speak up*?**
   a) while you are studying in a library
   b) at a rock concert
   c) when you're trying to get to sleep

2 **Is *speak up* the right thing to say in these situations? Choose the best phrase for each.**
   a) *Speak up!/Don't speak so loudly!* Why are you whispering?
   b) *Speak up!/Start again!* You're not making any sense!
   c) *Speak up!/Don't speak so loudly!* You know I'm going deaf!
   d) *Speak up!/Speed up!* You're talking much too slowly!
   e) *Speak up!/Speak more quietly!* There's no need to shout!

   Now check your answers by looking at *speak up* on p. 108.

BUILD YOUR VOCABULARY

OTHER MEANINGS
Speak up can also mean 'to say what you think clearly and freely':
*Several of the players **spoke up** for their manager and said he should not resign.*
*It's time to **speak up** about (= say we do not like) these terrible housing conditions.*

TAKE UP *something*

FIRST MEANING

STUDY **Read these sentences carefully.**

- I didn't know you'd **taken up** cookery!
- He's **taken up** jogging in order to lose weight.
- She **took up** languages and now speaks Chinese quite well.
- I used to do a bit of writing and I'd like to **take** it **up** again.

CHECK **Use the sentences in the Study box to help you do these exercises.**

MEANING
Choose <u>three</u> of the words below to complete this meaning of *take up* something.

activity   pleasure   start   work

to .... to do a new ...., especially for ....

GRAMMAR
Which of these are grammatically possible?
a) She took up sailing.
b) She took it up.
c) She took up it.
d) Sailing was taken up.

Now check your answers by looking at *take up sth* on p. 109.

PRACTISE

**1 Complete the sentences with the correct form of *take up* and one of
the objects below:**

aerobics   different instruments   it   one   smoking
a) Nigel recently .... at the local sports centre.
b) He advises parents and children on the dangers of ....
c) Rather than all of us playing the flute, I think we should ....
d) I had never been fishing before, but I have now .... and am
enjoying it.
e) I never had the time for a hobby, even if I had wanted to ....

2 Correct any errors in the following:
a) She decided to take up walk in order to keep fit.
b) I believe she took up the violin at the age of 4.
c) I was no good at rugby so I take up rowing.
d) There are lots of hobbies you can take them up.

Now check your answers by looking at *take up sth* on p. 109.

BUILD YOUR VOCABULARY

OPPOSITES
➤ *give up; give up something*

96

TAKE UP *something*

SECOND MEANING

> **STUDY** Read these sentences carefully.
>
> - The equipment is expensive and **takes up** a lot of space.
> - I'm sorry to **take up** so much of your time.
> - Looking for a place to live has been **taking up** all my time recently.
> - The whole day has **been taken up** with making phone calls.

CHECK Use the sentences in the Study box to help you do these exercises.

MEANING
Choose the best verb to complete this meaning of *take something up*.

arrange   be   fill   organize

to .... a particular amount of space or time

GRAMMAR
Which of these are grammatically possible?
a) The television takes up a lot of room.
b) The television takes a lot of room up.
c) A lot of room is taken up.

Now check your answers by looking at *take up sth* on p. 109.

PRACTISE

I Complete these sentences with either a <u>positive</u> or <u>negative</u> form of *take up* in a suitable tense.
a) This sleeping bag rolls up really small so it .... much space in my rucksack.
b) I wish you didn't have to work so much. It .... too much of your time.
c) I'm sure he won't mind helping you, as long as you .... too much of his time.
d) He found that most of his time .... with looking after the children.
e) Once we folded the chairs up, they hardly .... any room.

2 In <u>one</u> of these sentences the verb *take up* is not used correctly. Can you find and correct the mistake?
a) The annual report takes up nearly thirty pages.
b) The new flat screen monitors are very popular as they take up so little space.
c) The main problem with this software is that it takes up too much disk space.
d) What space there was had been took up by two long tables.

Now check your answers by looking at *take up sth* on p. 109.

TURN UP

STUDY Read these sentences carefully.

- He **turned up** late, as usual.
- The taxi didn't **turn up** so we had to walk.
- By the time I **turned up** at the party, most people had already left.
- Around 5,000 people **turned up** to celebrate the start of the new year.
- You don't need to book a place on the course - just **turn up**.

CHECK Use the sentences in the Study box to help you do these exercises.

MEANING
Which two of the following are close to this meaning of *turn up*?

a) to leave   **b)** to arrive   **c)** to appear   **d)** to go

GRAMMAR
Which of these are grammatically possible?

a) He turned up.
b) He turned up the party.
c) He was turned up.

Now check your answers by looking at *turn up* on p. 110.

PRACTISE

1 You arranged to meet somebody, but did he turn up? Answer *yes* or *no* for each of the following:
a) He eventually arrived.
b) I had to go on my own.
c) I was so glad to see him.
d) He's so unreliable!
e) He brought a friend with him.

2 Complete the following sentences in an appropriate way, using a form of *turn up* and any other necessary information:
a) I'm glad Maria came to the party. What time ....?
b) I was hoping John would come, but ....
c) I don't think James will be there on time. He always ....
d) I'm sorry I'm so late. The bus ....

Now check your answers by looking at *turn up* on p. 110.

BUILD YOUR VOCABULARY

SYNONYMS
The verb **show up** means the same and is used in the same way, but is more informal:
*Did Mark **show up** at the restaurant last night?*

TURN *something* UP

STUDY Read these sentences carefully.

- You'll have to **turn** the volume **up** - she's a bit deaf.
- I closed the window and **turned up** the heating.
- I can't hear the radio. Can you **turn** it **up**?
- The television **was turned up** so loud that she couldn't hear him shouting.

CHECK Use the sentences in the Study box to help you do these exercises.

MEANING
Complete the meaning of this use of *turn something up* using the words below:

increase   equipment   noise   controls

to adjust the .... on a piece of .... in order to ....
the amount of heat, ... or power that is produced

GRAMMAR
Which of these are grammatically possible?
a) I turned up.
b) I turned the radio up.
c) I turned up the radio.
d) I turned it up.
e) The radio was turned up.

Now check your answers by looking at *turn sth up* on p. 110.

PRACTISE

1 What does *it* refer to in each sentence? Choose from the words below.
  Use each object only once.

the music   the gas   the television   the radio
a) She turned it up and everybody started dancing.
b) He always turns it up loud when his favourite programmes are on.
c) If we turn it up any higher we'll burn the rice.
d) Don't turn it up - I only want to watch the pictures.

2 Complete the following sentences in an appropriate way, using *turn something up* and an object (a noun or a pronoun):
a) We can't hear the music. ....!
b) It's very cold in here. Do you mind if ....?
c) She wanted the chicken to cook quickly, so she ....

Now check your answers by looking at *turn sth up* on p. 110.

BUILD YOUR VOCABULARY

OPPOSITES
The opposite of **turn something up** is **turn something down**:
*I was hot so I **turned** the heating **down**, but he said he was cold and **turned** it back **up**.*

WAKE UP; WAKE *somebody* UP

STUDY Read these sentences carefully.

- He's always in a bad mood when he **wakes up**.
- Please try not to **wake** the baby **up**. I've only just got him to sleep.
- Sh! You'll **wake up** the whole family if you don't keep quiet.
- Will you **wake** me **up** at 7 o'clock tomorrow, please?
- We **were woken up** by the sound of breaking glass.

CHECK Use the sentences in the Study box to help you do these exercises.

MEANING
What is the opposite of *wake up*? Choose <u>one</u> answer.
a) get out of bed   **b)** lie down   **c)** go to sleep

GRAMMAR
Which of these are grammatically possible?

a) She woke up.
b) She woke her father up.
c) She woke up her father.
d) She woke him up.
e) She woke up him.
f) He was woken up.

Now check your answers by looking at *wake up; wake sb up* on p. 110.

PRACTISE

1 Respond to the following in an appropriate way, using the verb *wake up* or *wake somebody up* in each case:
a) Did you sleep well last night?
    No, I ....
b) Is Dad still in bed?
    Yes. Don't ....

2 Are the following sentences grammatically correct? Correct any errors that you find.
a) It's 8 o'clock. Shall I wake Sarah up now?
b) Why do you always wake up me when you come home? Can't you be quieter?
c) She was waked up three times during the night by the noise outside.

Now check your answers by looking at *wake up; wake sb up* on p. 110.

BUILD YOUR VOCABULARY

RELATED WORDS
adjective: **wake-up** *(This is only used before a noun.)*
A telephone call that is intended to wake you up is a **wake-up call**.

be 'up to sb
to be somebody's responsibility or duty; to be left to somebody to decide
CHECK
Meaning: 1 b 2 a
Grammar: b, d
PRACTISE
1 a) It is up to students to find their own accommodation. b) It is up to the prosecution lawyer to prove that somebody is guilty in court. c) I don't mind where we go - it's up to you. d) Jenny can go to the party if she likes - it's up to her. 2 a) That's up to my boss. b) No, it's up to me to keep my room tidy/to tidy my room. c) That's up to the judge.

be 'up to sth
to be busy doing something, especially something bad
CHECK
Meaning: 1 b 2 something bad
Grammar: a NOTE You can sometimes use the verb **get** instead of **be**: *What did you get up to last night?* **Be up to** can also mean 'to be as good as people expect' or 'to be able to do something': *Was your meal up to standard?* ◇ *In her condition she wasn't really up to walking a long way.*
PRACTISE
1 a) ii b) iii c) i d) iv 2 *Suggested Answers:* a) So, what were you up to last night? b) What has he been up to (to get so dirty)? c) Do you think the children are up to something?

,blow 'up; ,blow sb/sth 'up
to explode or be destroyed by an explosion; to kill somebody or destroy something with a bomb or an explosion
CHECK
Meaning: 1 a 2 a
Grammar: a, b, c, d, f
PRACTISE
a) The demonstrators threatened to blow up the offices if... b) ... when the old heating boiler blew up. c) ... and blew it up. d) An attempt was made to blow up the company director, but...

,blow sth 'up
to fill something with air or gas
CHECK
Meaning: 2 a, b, d
Grammar: a, b, c, e
PRACTISE
Suggested Answers: a) No, we haven't blown up the balloons. b) Yes. They were flat so I blew them up.

,break 'down
to stop working because of a fault
CHECK
Meaning: b, c
Grammar: a, c
PRACTISE
1 a) broken b) breaks down c) broke d) broken 2

Suggested Answers: a) Because the washing machine has broken down. b) Yes, it never breaks down.

,break 'up
(of a relationship) to come to an end; (of people) to end a relationship; to stop working together
CHECK
Meaning: a) comes to an end b) end a relationship
Grammar: a, c, d NOTE You can also use the pattern *break sb up*: *She doesn't want me to marry him and is always trying to break us up.*
PRACTISE
1 a) Her marriage broke up in 1985... b) Many bands break up... c) ...after she broke up with John. 2 No, they have broken up/they broke up a few weeks ago. ◇ Yes, they haven't broken up yet.

,bring sb 'up
to care for a child until he or she is grown up; to teach your child a particular way to behave
CHECK
Meaning: a, c
Grammar: a, b, c, e
PRACTISE
1 a) ...so his grandparents brought him up. b) Do you think parents should bring boys and girls up in the same way? c) I was brought up on a farm.

,call 'back; ,call sb 'back
to telephone somebody again; to telephone somebody who telephoned you earlier
CHECK
Meaning: b
Grammar: a, b, d
PRACTISE
Suggested Answers: a) ...so I called her back later. b) ...Can I call you back? c) ...and he called me back. d) ...but she hasn't called me back (yet).

,catch 'up; ,catch sb/sth 'up
to reach somebody or something ahead of you by going faster than them or it
CHECK
Meaning: a, b, e
Grammar: a, b, d, e NOTE The pattern c) *She caught up Tom* is possible but rare.
PRACTISE
a) ...and said he would catch me up. b) She was driving so fast that I couldn't catch up (with her). c) ...and let him catch up (with me). d) ... nobody will be able to catch up (with you).

,check 'in; ,check sb/sth 'in
when you check in, you go to an official desk at a hotel or an airport and tell somebody that you have arrived; when somebody checks you in they take your name when you arrive at a hotel or an airport; when somebody checks luggage in, they either leave it or accept it to be put on a plane, etc.
CHECK
Meaning: 1 b 2 a

Grammar: a, b, c, d, f NOTE The pattern *check into sth* can also be used: *We checked into our hotel.*
PRACTISE
a) We checked in at Heathrow at 2 p.m.... **b)** ✔
c) ✔ **d)** After checking in and …

‚check 'out; ‚check 'out of sth
to leave a hotel, a hospital, etc. where you have been staying
CHECK
Meaning: 1 b, d, e 2 a, b, d
Grammar: a, c
PRACTISE
a) check out **b)** checked out of **c)** check out **d)** checked out **e)** had checked out of

‚check sb/sth **'out**
to find out if something is true or correct, or if somebody is honest, truthful, reliable, etc.
CHECK
Meaning: **a)** honest, reliable **b)** true, correct, acceptable
Grammar: a, b, c, e NOTE The pattern *check people out* is much less frequent.
PRACTISE
a) I think we should check out his story/check his story out. **b)** The police checked out the names and addresses. **c)** Can you check something out for me? **d)** Potential employees are always thoroughly checked out.

‚cheer 'up; ‚cheer sb/yourself **'up**
to become, or to make somebody or yourself, happier or more cheerful
CHECK
Meaning: a
Grammar: a, b, d, e, f
PRACTISE
1 *Suggested Answers:* **a)** Why don't you cheer her up by taking her to see a movie? **b)** Yes. He has cheered up a lot. **c)** Cheer up! It'll soon be spring.

‚come a'cross
to meet or find somebody or something by chance, without having planned or thought about it
CHECK
Meaning: 2 a
Grammar: b, d
PRACTISE
a) Did you come across anything interesting …? **b)** …My father came across it in the library. **c)** This is a recipe that I came across in a French dictionary of cooking. **d)** James is the strangest person I've ever come across! **e)** Have you come across a girl called…?

‚come 'on
used to encourage somebody to do something, to show that you do not believe what somebody has said or to disagree with somebody
CHECK
Meaning: b
Grammar: a NOTE This verb is only used in the form *Come on.*

PRACTISE
1 a, b 2 **a)** Come on! **b)** Absolutely! **c)** Come on! **d)** Come on! **e)** Come down!

‚come 'round
to come to somebody's home to see them for a short time
CHECK
Meaning: b
Grammar: a, c
PRACTISE
1 **a)** My parents usually come round to our place on Sundays. **b)** …, do come round for coffee. **c)** … Can I come round and/to use yours? **d)** … Some friends are coming round (to my house). 2 Would you like to come round for lunch on Saturday?

‚cut 'down
to eat, drink or use less of something, usually to improve your health or your situation
CHECK
Grammar: a, c
PRACTISE
1 *Suggested Answers:* You should cut down on junk food. ◊ You smoke too much. You should cut down. 2 I wish I could cut down on chocolate. ◊ I drink too much coffee. I'm trying to cut down.

‚cut sb **'off**
to interrupt a telephone conversation by breaking the connection
CHECK
Grammar: a, c, e NOTE This verb is usually used in the passive.
PRACTISE
a) They were suddenly cut off. **b)** Operator, we've been cut off. **c)** I'm so sorry. My son cut us off.

‚cut sb/sth **'off**
FIRST MEANING
to separate somebody, something or yourself physically or socially from other people or things
CHECK
Grammar: a, b, c, e, g
PRACTISE
1 a, c 2 **a)** We are often cut off in the winter because of bad weather. **b)** You can't expect me to cut myself off completely from my friends. **c)** ✔ **d)** The country had been cut off from all contact with the outside world.
SECOND MEANING
to stop the supply of gas, water, electricity, etc. to somebody's home
CHECK
Meaning: 1 c 2 a, b, d, e, g
Grammar: a, b, d NOTE You can also use the pattern *cut the electricity supply off*, but this is less frequent. *Cut sb/sth off* is often used in the passive in this meaning.
PRACTISE
1 **a)** Because our telephone has been cut off. **b)** The company will cut you/the electricity off. **c)** Because the gas has been cut off. 2 **a)** ✔ **b)** She didn't pay the bill so they cut her off. **c)** ✔ **d)** They

were wearing coats and scarves as the electricity had been cut off.

,do sth 'up
to fasten or close something
CHECK
Meaning: 1 b 2 a, c, e
Grammar: a, b, c, e NOTE You can also use the pattern: *This dress does up at the back.*
PRACTISE
a) Yes, if you do it up/do the buttons up/do up the buttons. b) ... I couldn't do them/the zip up! c) ... Your laces were not done up.

,drop sb/sth 'off
to stop and let somebody get out of a vehicle; to deliver something to a place, often when you are on the way to somewhere else
CHECK
Meaning: 1 a 2 b
Grammar: a, b, c, e
PRACTISE
1 a) Could you drop me off outside the hotel, please? b) ...Shall I drop your books off/drop off your books for you? c) Where shall I drop you off? ... 2 a) ✔ b) ✔ c) ... - why don't you ask her to drop you off?

,fall 'over
to be unable to stay standing and fall to the ground
CHECK
Grammar: a, d
PRACTISE
1 b, c 2 a, c, d

,fill sth 'in
to complete a document (for example a form or a questionnaire) by writing the necessary information on it
CHECK
Grammar: a, b, d NOTE You can also use the pattern *fill the form in*, but this is rare.
PRACTISE
a) Once you have filled in your personal details, ...
b) ...and here are some notes to help you fill it in.
c) Thank you for filling in our questionnaire. ... d) He filled in her name on the invitation... e) About 35% of people had filled in their forms incorrectly.

,fill sth 'up
to make a container completely full
CHECK
Grammar: a, b, c, e NOTE You can also use *fill up* with this pattern: *The boat was filling up with water.* ◊ *After 8 o'clock, the restaurant began to fill up.*
PRACTISE
a) She...and filled it up again. b) ...,fill the jug up/fill up the jug from the tap. c) ....I only filled it up last week! d) You don't need to fill the kettle/teapot up just to make one cup of tea!

,find 'out; ,find sth 'out
to learn a fact, a piece of information or the truth about somebody or something
CHECK
Meaning: a
Grammar: a, c, d NOTE *I found the truth out* is also possible, but rare. The passive is almost never used.
PRACTISE
a) I want you to find out who he is. b) Can you find out where he lives? c) Please find out when he started following me. d) I must find out why he is following me. e) I need to find out how he knows my name. f) I have to find out what he wants.

,get 'in; ,get 'in sth
to enter or go inside something; to succeed in entering a place, especially a building
CHECK
Meaning: 1 a, c, d 2 c
Grammar: a, b, d NOTE When you use an object, you can also use the pattern *get into something.* Sometimes this is less informal than **get in sth**. *They all got in/into the car and it drove off.* ◊ *It's late. Hurry up and get into bed now.*
PRACTISE
a) Quick! Get in (the car) and fasten your seatbelt! b) She got in the cab/taxi and.... c) ...you can get in free on Sundays. d) ...I'll go under the bed and you get in the cupboard/closet!

,get 'off; ,get 'off sth
to leave a bus, train, plane, etc. that you are travelling in
CHECK
Meaning: 1 a 2 a, b, d, e, f, h
Grammar: a, c, e
PRACTISE
a) ...and they wouldn't let us get off the plane. b) You can ask the driver where to get off/where you should get off. c) ...I got off (the bus) at the wrong stop and had to walk. d) ... Get off (your bike) at once!

,get 'on
to have a friendly relationship with somebody
CHECK
Grammar: a, b, d
PRACTISE
a) iv b) i c) iii d) ii

,get 'on; ,get 'on sth
to get into a bus, train, plane, etc.
CHECK
Meaning: 1 b 2 a, b, d, e, f, h
Grammar: a, b, d
PRACTISE
a) He got on his bike and cycled off.... b) ...before they let us get on the plane. c) ...,so we'd better get on it. d) I got on a bus that took me straight to the airport.... e) ... Shall we get on it?

,get 'out; ,get 'out of sth
to leave or go out of a place such as a car, a lift, a room or a house; to manage to find a way out of a place

CHECK
Meaning: 1 a, c, d, e 2 c
Grammar: a, b, d
PRACTISE
a) …but then lots of people got out at the next station. **b)** …and it couldn't get out. **c)** Let's get out here…. **d)** I usually try to get out of the office for an hour at lunchtime.

,get 'out of sth
to avoid a responsibility or duty; to not do something that you ought to do
CHECK
Meaning: c
Grammar: b, d, e
PRACTISE
1 **a)** No. **b)** Yes. **c)** Yes. **d)** No. 2 **a)** …we can't get out of it. **b)** …and tried to get out of paying. **c)** …but there was no getting out of them. **d)** …I don't think I can get out of it.

,get 'over sb/sth
to return to your usual state of health or happiness after an illness, a shock, the end of a relationship, etc.
CHECK
Meaning: 1 b 2 a, c
Grammar: b, d
PRACTISE
a) …but she soon got over her homesickness. **b)** …as I was (still) getting over bronchitis. **c)** When I had got over the shock… **d)** He was very ill, but he seems to have got over it now. **e)** We spent the first day of our holiday getting over the long flight.

,get 'up; ,get sb **'up**
to get out of bed; to make somebody get out of bed
CHECK
Meaning: b
Grammar: a, b, d NOTE You can also use *get yourself up: Jack had to get himself up and off to school.*
PRACTISE
1 *Suggested Answers:* **a)** I usually get up at… **b)** At the weekend I get up at…/I don't get up until… **c)** I got up at… **d)** I think I'll get up at…/I ought to get up at… 2 *Suggested Answers:* What are you doing still in bed? Get up and do something useful.

,give sth **a'way**
to give something to somebody as a gift
CHECK
Meaning: c
Grammar: a, b, c, e
PRACTISE
a) Dave has decided to give all his money away/give away all his money to charity. **b)** …They were giving them away free at the market. **c)** …so I sold four of them and gave the rest away/gave away the rest. **d)** … - he gave away his old car/gave his old car away when he bought the new one. **e)** …I've decided to give everything away.

,give sth **'out**
to hand something to a lot of people

CHECK
Meaning: b
Grammar: a, b, c, e
PRACTISE
a) She gave out invitations to her wedding…. **b)** The teacher…started giving out exam papers/giving exam papers out to all the students. **c)** The relief organizations…were giving out free food/giving free food out to the refugees. **d)** …Do you need any help with giving out leaflets/giving leaflets out?

,give 'up; ,give 'up sth
FIRST MEANING
to stop trying to do something, usually because it is too difficult
CHECK
Grammar: a, b, c, f NOTE You can also use the pattern *give the attempt up*, but this is less frequent.
PRACTISE
1 **a)** ii **b)** i **c)** iv **d)** iii 2 *Suggested Answers:* **a)** Don't give up - I know you can do it! **b)** In the end, I gave up trying to find him./I couldn't find him and in the end I gave up (the search). **c)** He was exhausted but he wouldn't give up.
SECOND MEANING
to stop doing or having something that you consider unhealthy
CHECK
Meaning: b
Grammar: a, b, c, f NOTE You can also use the pattern *give coffee up*, but this is less frequent.
PRACTISE
1 *Suggested Answers:* **a)** …I (know I) ought to give up. **b)** …I've given up (drinking) coffee./I'm trying to give up (drinking) coffee.

,go 'off
FIRST MEANING
(of a weapon, etc.) to be fired; to explode
CHECK
Meaning: 1 **a)** explodes **b)** fired **c)** loud noise 2 b, c, e
Grammar: a
PRACTISE
Suggested Answers: **a)** …It sounded as if a bomb had gone off. **b)** …They might go off before you are ready. **c)** …My alarm didn't go off. **d)** The thieves ran away when the (burglar) alarm went off.
SECOND MEANING
if food or drink goes off, it becomes bad and not fit to eat or drink
CHECK
Meaning: 1 a, b, d 2 a, b, d, f
Grammar: a
PRACTISE
a) We can't, the chicken has gone off. **b)** I'm afraid the salmon has gone off too. **c)** No, they've gone off. **d)** We can't, the milk's gone off.

,go 'on
FIRST MEANING
(of a situation or a state of affairs) to continue to happen or exist without changing; (of a person) to continue an activity without stopping

CHECK
Meaning: **a)** ii **b)** i
Grammar: a, b, c, d
PRACTISE
I a) ii **b)** i **c)** iii **2 a)** …Things can't go on as they
are. **b)** …everybody just went on talking/went on
with what they were doing.
SECOND MEANING
to take place; to happen
CHECK
Meaning: b
Grammar: a, c NOTE This verb is usually used in
the progressive tenses.
PRACTISE
I a) iii **b)** v **c)** iv **d)** ii **e)** i **2** *Suggested Answers:* **a)**
…What's going on? **b)** …There's nothing going
on/There must be something going on. **c)** …and I
never discovered what had been going on.

,go 'out
FIRST MEANING
to leave your house to go to social events
CHECK
Meaning: b
Grammar: a
PRACTISE
I a) Yes, we went out for a special meal. **b)** I usu-
ally go out with my friends. **c)** No, he's gone out to
a party. **2** *Suggested Answers:* **a)** I never/sometimes
go out on Friday and Saturday evenings. **b)** I didn't
go out last night. **c)** My parents often/always let me
go out (with friends) when I was young
SECOND MEANING
(especially of young people) to spend time
with somebody and have a romantic
relationship with them
CHECK
Grammar: a, b, c
PRACTISE
I a) Kate and Sam have been going out (together)
/Kate has been going out with Sam for three years.
b) How long did those two go out together? **c)**
They went out (together) for years before they
finally got married. **d)** Are you going out with
anyone at the moment?
THIRD MEANING
(of a fire or a light) to stop burning or shining
CHECK
Meaning: **a)** shining **b)** burning
Grammar: a
PRACTISE
I a) the fire **b)** the flame **c)** the candle **d)** the
torch **2** *Suggested Answers:* **a)** Because the fire has
gone out. **b)** Nobody. They just went out.

,grow 'up
to become an adult; to spend the time when
you are a child in a particular place or a
particular way
CHECK
Meaning: a
Grammar: a, c

PRACTISE
I a) grown **b)** grown **c)** grew up **2** *Suggested*
Answers: **a)** I grew up in… **b)** I wanted to be a …
when I grew up.

,hang 'up; ,hang 'up sth
to end a telephone conversation, often very
suddenly, by putting down the part of the
telephone that you speak into or switching the
telephone off
CHECK
Meaning: **I** c **2** b
Grammar: a, c, e NOTE The pattern *hang the phone*
up is also possible but very rare.
PRACTISE
a) …, or shall I hang up when we've finished? **b)**
…the caller hung up immediately. **c)** …'Nothing.
He hung up on me!' **d)** 'Sorry, wrong number,' she
said, hanging up the phone.

,have sth 'on; have ,got sth 'on
to be wearing something
CHECK
Meaning: **I** a **2** a, d
Grammar: a, b, c NOTE This verb is not used in the
progressive tenses.
PRACTISE
I a) Today I've got/I have my favourite sweater on.
b) ✔ **c)** I was cold because I hadn't got/didn't have
a coat on.

,hold 'on
used to ask somebody to wait for a short time
CHECK
Meaning: b
Grammar: a, c NOTE This verb is usually used in
informal spoken English and in the form *Hold on.*
PRACTISE
I b **2** *Suggested Answers:* **a)** Hold on (a minute) - I
need to make a quick phone call. **b)** Let's hold on a
few minutes and see if any more students arrive.

,hold sb/sth 'up
to block or delay the progress of somebody or
something
CHECK
Grammar: a, b, c, e NOTE The pattern *hold the*
meeting up is not very common. This verb is often
used in the passive.
PRACTISE
I a) …He's been held up in Chicago on business.
b) …They (must) have been held up in traffic. **c)**
… in case they were/the boat was held up by gales.
d) …, and traffic was held up for over an hour. **2 a)**
I held things up for an hour… **b)** ✔ **c)** …, the
trains are held up.

,keep 'up
to move at the same rate or speed as
somebody or something
CHECK
Meaning: a
Grammar: a, c
PRACTISE
I a) …Please try to keep up (with us)! **b)** …I can't

keep up (with you)! **c)** ...Joe would have difficulty keeping up (with us). **2 a)** catch up **b)** catch up **c)** keep up

leave sb/sth **'out;** **leave** sb/sth **'out of** sth
to not include somebody or something, either accidentally or on purpose
CHECK
Meaning: **1** b **2** c
Grammar: a, b, c, e
PRACTISE
a) ...and don't leave out any details/leave any details out! **b)** It seemed wrong to leave Daisy out so she came along too. **c)** ...but I left out the '0'/I left the '0' out. **d)** David was left out of the team....

let sb **'down**
to fail to help or support somebody in the way that they hope or expect
CHECK
Meaning: a
Grammar: a, b, c, e NOTE Pattern b), *He let down his parents,* is less frequent.
PRACTISE
1 b **2 a)** He never lets anybody down. **b)** If I fail, I'll feel that I've let my parents down.

log 'off; **log 'off** sth
to perform the actions that allow you to finish using a computer system
CHECK
Grammar: a, c, e NOTE This verb is very flexible. It can also be used with these patterns: *Click this button to log off the current user.*(= log off sb, log you off) ◊ *This button will log you off the website.* (= log sb off sth)
PRACTISE
a) Teenagers are logging off the Internet in millions... **b)** You might have to wait until one of the other users has logged off. **c)** You have just logged off our website....

log 'on; **log 'onto** sth
to perform the actions that allow you to begin using a computer system
CHECK
Grammar: a, c, e NOTE This verb is very flexible. It can also be used with these patterns: *The system was unable to log you on.* (= log sb on) ◊ *This will automatically log you onto the website.* (= log sb onto sth)
PRACTISE
a) Every evening she logs onto the Internet.... **b)** You can't log onto the system without a user name.... **c)** Press CTRL + ALT + DELETE to log on.

look 'after sb/sth/yourself
to make sure that somebody or something is safe; to take care of somebody, something or yourself
CHECK
Meaning: c, e
Grammar: b, d, e

PRACTISE
a) ...the nurses loked after him very well. **b)** ...He's quite old enough to look after himself. **c)** ...She loves looking after children. **d)** ...I wish you would look after your clothes.

'look for sb/sth
to search for somebody or something, either because you have lost them/it or because you need them/it
CHECK
Meaning: b
Grammar: a, c NOTE The passive is rare.
PRACTISE
1 a) ...Yes, I'm looking for a blue shirt. **b)** ...I've been looking for it everywhere. **c)** Clare was..., looking for her contact lenses. **d)** She was frantically looking for her son, ... **e)** ...I'm going to look for an apartment in the centre of town. **2 a)** ✔ **b)** ✔ **c)** Sarah lost her keys, so we spent ages looking for them all over the house.

look 'forward to sth
to feel excited about something that is going to happen in the future
CHECK
Meaning: b
Grammar: a, b, d NOTE You can also use *look forward to* in the passive, but this is not very common: *Her visit was eagerly looked forward to.*
PRACTISE
1 a) I'm looking forward to the party very much.... **b)** ...I'm really looking forward to meeting him. **c)** ✔ **d)** ...so we always looked forward to it.

look sth **'up**
to search for a word or some information in a book or on a computer
CHECK
Grammar: a, b, c, e NOTE The passive is also possible but very rare.
PRACTISE
1 a) ✔ **b)** I usually look up new words/look new words up in a bilingual dictionary. **c)** ✔ **d)** ✔ **2 a)** Every time I try to look something up,.... **b)** Why don't you look up her number/look her number up in the phone book...? **c)** ...I looked it up on the timetable.

make sth **'up**
to invent something, often in order to deceive somebody
CHECK
Meaning: c
Grammar: a, b, d NOTE The pattern *He made the story up* is also possible but less frequent.
PRACTISE
1 *Suggested Answers:* **a)** No, I think he made it all up. **b)** No, it's (been) made up. **c)** Oh, I just made one/something up. **d)** I promise I'm not making it/this up. **2 a)** ✔ **b)** Most of what had been

written about her in the papers had been made up.
c) He can't have made up all that stuff…, can he?

ˌown ˈup; ˌown ˈup to sth
to admit that you are the person responsible
for something that has happened
CHECK
Meaning: a
Grammar: a, c, d, f
PRACTISE
I a, d 2 a) owned up to b) owned up c) owns up
d) owning up e) owned up to f) own up to

ˌpick sb/sth ˈup
FIRST MEANING
to take hold of and lift somebody or something
CHECK
Meaning: c
Grammar: a, b, c, e
PRACTISE
a) …, so I picked it up for him. b) …, you have to
pick up a card/pick a card up from the pile. c) … I
could only just pick her up. d) I spent a few
minutes picking up her clothes/picking her clothes
up off the floor… e) Did you pick up my credit
card/pick my credit card up by mistake? …
SECOND MEANING
if you pick somebody up, you go to their home
or a place you have arranged and take them
somewhere in your car; if you pick something
up, you obtain or collect it
CHECK
Meaning: I b 2 a
Grammar: a, b, c, e
PRACTISE
a) …I have to pick my son (or daughter) up/pick
up my son (or daughter) from school. b) We need
to pick the tickets up/pick up the tickets from the
Box Office. c) …I can't pick you up until eight. d)
He had to…pick up some things for the weekend.

ˌput sth aˈway
to put something in a box, a drawer, etc.
because you have finished using it
CHECK
Meaning: c
Grammar: a, b, c, e
PRACTISE
I a) You'd better put the cakes away/put away the
cakes before I eat them all! b) …or shall I put it
away? c) Stop playing and put your toys away now,
Tim. … d) I think I'll put the car away in the
garage… e) …Why can't you put them away? 2
Suggested Answers: a) No, don't put it away yet. /
Yes, you can put it away now. b) I've just put it
away/It's been put away (in the fridge).

ˌput sb/sth ˈdown
to place somebody or something that you are
holding on the floor or another surface
CHECK
Grammar: a, b, c, e
PRACTISE
Suggested Answers: a) The book was so good that I

couldn't put it down. b) …Why doesn't she put
some of them down? c) The police told the
robbers to put down their guns/put their guns
down. d) …You can put him/her down now.

ˌput sb ˈoff; ˌput sb ˈoff sth
FIRST MEANING
to make somebody stop liking or being
interested in somebody or something
CHECK
Grammar: a, b, d, e, f NOTE The pattern *It put off
John* is possible but very rare.
PRACTISE
a) The accident put James off riding a bike for a
long time. b) Don't be put off by the cost of the
book. c) His political views put me off him.
SECOND MEANING
to disturb somebody who is trying to give all
their attention to something
CHECK
Meaning: a
Grammar: a, c, d, e
PRACTISE
I a) …Doesn't it/the noise put you off? b) …They
will put me off. c) …I can turn the radio off if it
puts you off. 2 a) …I mustn't let anything put me
off my work this week. b) ✔ c) The children
all…tried to put the teacher off. d) The noise of
the traffic was putting her off,…

ˌput sth ˈoff
to change something to a later date or time
CHECK
Meaning: b
Grammar: a, b, c, e
PRACTISE
I a) Can we put it off until tomorrow? b) ,,. - it
cannot be put off any longer. c) I always put my
work off/put off my work until the last minute.

ˌput sth ˈon
to put an item of clothing on your body
CHECK
Meaning: I b 2 b, e
Grammar: a, b, c NOTE **Put sth on** can also mean
the same as **turn sth on**, especially in British
English: *It's rather dark here. Can you put the light on?*
PRACTISE
I a) wear b) wearing c) put on 2 a) Why don't
you put your jacket on/put on your jacket? b)
Don't forget to put on a tie/put a tie on!

ˌput sb ˈout
to make trouble, problems or extra work for
somebody
CHECK
Meaning: b
Grammar: a, c
PRACTISE
I a) ✘ b) ✔ c) ✔ d) ✘ 2 a) I hope our arriving
late didn't put you out at all. b) Would it put you
out too much if he came to stay for a day or two?

ˌput sth ˈout
to stop something burning

CHECK
Meaning: a
Grammar: a, b, c, e
PRACTISE
1 a) iv **b)** iii **c)** ii **d)** i **2** *Suggested Answers:* **a)** ...to put out fires/put fires out. **b)** ...if he would put his cigarette out/put out his cigarette. **c)** ...before it was put out.

,put 'up with sb/sth
to accept somebody or something that is annoying, difficult or unpleasant, without complaining
CHECK
Meaning: b
Grammar: a, c, e
PRACTISE
1 a) the weather **b)** the noise **c)** the problem **d)** the dust **e)** this behaviour **2** *Suggested Answers:* **b)** Because I can't put up with the way he talks to us. **c)** Because I couldn't put up with the noise and the traffic. **d)** No, but I (can) put up with it!

,run 'out; ,run 'out of sth
if a supply of something runs out, it is used up; if a person or a machine runs out of a supply of something, they finish it or use it all up
CHECK
Meaning: supply, none, used
Grammar: a, b, d
PRACTISE
1 *Suggested Answers:* **a)** Because funds ran out. **b)** You can't. We've run out of coffee/milk. **c)** I think it's run out. **d)** No. I've run out of money. **2 a)** ✔ **b)** You have run out of space on the disk. **c)** ... he soon ran out of film. **d)** ... as the white had run out. **e)** ✔ **f)** ... they're running out of ideas.

,sell 'out; ,sell 'out of sth; be ,sold 'out
if tickets for a concert, a game, etc. sell out or are sold out, they are all sold and there are none left; if somebody sells out of something or is sold out, they have sold all of it and have nothing left
CHECK
Meaning: **a)** all, none **b)** all, nothing
Grammar: a, c, d NOTE You can also use the pattern *be sold out of sth: They are already sold out of tickets.*
PRACTISE
Suggested Answers: **a)** No, they were sold out/the shop had sold out. **b)** Because they will sell out quickly. **c)** I'm afraid we've sold out.

,set 'off
to begin a journey
CHECK
Grammar: a
PRACTISE
1 a) After breakfast they set off up the mountain. **b)** Do you want something to eat before you set off for work? **c)** He finally set off on the first stage of his round-the-world trip. **d)** Every morning she sets off at 6 a.m..... **e)** ...We didn't set off until 8

o'clock! **2** *Suggested Answers:* **a)** I set off for college at 7.30 a.m. **b)** We should set off at 9 a.m.

,set sth 'up
to create something or start a business, an organization, etc.
CHECK
Meaning: b
Grammar: a, b, c, e NOTE It is also possible to use the pattern *he set up*, but only in sentences with other phrases such as *in business, on his own*, etc: *He set up in business in a town near Oxford.*
PRACTISE
1 b) When did he set it up? **c)** Why did he set up his own company? **d)** Will he set up another one?

,settle 'down
to start to have a calmer way of life, without many changes, especially living in one place
CHECK
Meaning: a, c, e
Grammar: a
PRACTISE
Suggested Answers: **a)** When are you going to settle down? **b)** Jim! I never thought he'd (get married and) settle down! **c)** Isn't it time he settled down and got a job/had a career? **d)** I don't want to settle down (with a career) just yet.

,slow 'down; ,slow sb/sth 'down
to go, or to make somebody or something go, at a slower speed
CHECK
Meaning: b
Grammar: a, b, c, d, f
PRACTISE
a) bus **b)** heat **c)** economy **d)** roadworks **e)** horse

,sort sth 'out
to deal with a problem or a situation in a satisfactory way
CHECK
Grammar: a, b, c, e NOTE You can also say: *The problem sorted itself out.*
PRACTISE
a) Did you sort out the problem with the heating? **b)** Have they sorted out all the problems? **c)** Did you (manage to) sort out your timetable?

,speak 'up
used to ask somebody to speak louder
CHECK
Meaning: c
Grammar: a NOTE This verb is usually used in the form *Speak up!* in this meaning.
PRACTISE
1 b **2 a)** Speak up! **b)** Start again! **c)** Speak up! **d)** Speed up! **e)** Speak more quietly!

,take 'after sb
to look like or behave like an older member of your family
CHECK
Meaning: b, d, e
Grammar: b, d

PRACTISE
I a) ii b) iv c) iii d) v e) i

,take 'off
(of an aircraft, etc.) to leave the ground and begin to fly
CHECK
Meaning: 2 a, c
Grammar: a, b
PRACTISE
I a) ii b) iv c) i d) iii 2 *Suggested Answers:* Our plane was 2 hours late taking off.

,take sth 'off
to remove an item of clothing from your or somebody else's body
CHECK
Meaning: I a 2 d
Grammar: a, b, c, e
PRACTISE
b) Why don't you take your sweater off/take off your sweater? c) I always take it off when I wash my hands. d) No. That's why I haven't taken my coat off/taken off my coat.

,take 'up sth
FIRST MEANING
to start to do a new activity, especially for pleasure
CHECK
Grammar: a, b NOTE The pattern *take sailing up* is possible, but very rare.
PRACTISE
I a) Nigel recently took up aerobics.... b) He advises...on the dangers of taking up smoking. c) ...., I think we should take up different instruments. d) ..., but I have now taken it up and am enjoying it. e) I never had the time for a hobby, even if I had wanted to take one up. 2 a) She decided to take up walking in order to keep fit. b) ✔ c) I was no good at rugby so I took up rowing. d) There are lots of hobbies you can take up.
SECOND MEANING
to fill a particular amount of space or time
CHECK
Grammar: a, c
PRACTISE
I a) doesn't/won't take up b) takes up c) don't take up d) was taken up e) took up 2 a) ✔ b) ✔ c) ✔ d) What space there was had been taken up by two long tables.

,tell sb 'off
to speak angrily to somebody, especially a child, because they have done something wrong
CHECK
Meaning: a
Grammar: a, c, e
PRACTISE
I a) ...she'll tell you off. b) Why are you always telling me off?... c) She told the children off... d) The teacher...told everyone off!

,throw something a'way
to get rid of something that has no use or that you no longer need
CHECK
Meaning: b
Grammar: a, b, c, e
PRACTISE
b) Throw them away then. c) ..., so don't throw it away. d) ..., but (you should) throw away the tie/throw the tie away.

,turn sb/sth 'down
to reject or refuse somebody or something
CHECK
Meaning: I a 2 a, b, d, f
Grammar: a, b, c, e, f
PRACTISE
a) Every record company had turned the band down so... b) ... when the Council turned down the plans for a larger school. c) Early in his career he (had) turned down the chance of.... d) Sadly, he had to turn down a place on a graduate course when... e) ...she couldn't imagine any woman turning him down.

,turn sth 'down
to adjust the controls on a piece of equipment in order to reduce the amount of heat, noise or light that is produced
CHECK
Grammar: b, c, d, e NOTE The pattern *turn down sth* is less common than *turn sth down*.
PRACTISE
Suggested Answers: a) Can you turn the music down? b) Do you mind if I turn the heating down a bit? c) ...but the sound had been turned down. d) ...so she turned the gas/heat down. e) ...so he put on some music and turned the lights down low

,turn sth 'off
to stop the flow of electricity, gas or water by moving a switch or pressing a button
CHECK
Grammar: a, b, c, e
PRACTISE
I a) I agree. Let's turn it off. b) No, don't turn it off yet. c) Sorry. I forgot to turn off the tap/turn the tap off. 2 a, b

,turn sth 'on
to start the flow of electricity, gas or water by moving a switch or pressing a button
CHECK
Grammar: a, b, c, e
PRACTISE
I a) We should turn on the heating/turn the heating on. b) It crashes every time I turn it on. c) ...so she turned on the car radio/turned the car radio on. 2 a) I forgot to turn on the answer machine/turn the answer machine on when.... b) ...you'll have to turn the hot water on now. c) ...Let me turn on the big light/turn the big light on for you. d) ✔

‚turn 'over; ‚turn sb/sth 'over

to change your position, or the position of somebody or something, so that the other side is facing outwards or upwards
CHECK
Meaning: a
Grammar: a, b, c, d, f
PRACTISE
I **a)** a card **b)** a question paper **c)** a hand **d)** a postcard **2 a)** He turned over,... **b)** ..., turning it over in her hands. **c)** Shall I turn the meat/egg/pancake over...?

‚turn 'up

to arrive
CHECK
Meaning: b, c
Grammar: a
PRACTISE
I **a)** Yes. **b)** No. **c)** Yes. **d)** No. **e)** Yes. **2 a)** ...What time did she turn up? **b)** ..., but he didn't turn up. **c)** ...He always turns up late. **d)** ...The bus didn't turn up./The bus turned up late.

‚turn sth 'up

to adjust the controls on a piece of equipment in order to increase the amount of heat, noise or power that is produced
CHECK
Grammar: b, c, d, e
PRACTISE
I **a)** the music **b)** the radio **c)** the gas **d)** the television **2 a)** ...Turn it up! **b)** ...Do you mind if I turn the heating up/turn up the heating a bit? **c)** ..., so she turned the gas/oven up.

‚wake 'up; ‚wake sb 'up

to stop sleeping; to make somebody stop sleeping
CHECK
Meaning: c
Grammar: a, b, c, d, f NOTE You can also use *wake yourself up: I fell out of bed and woke myself up.*
PRACTISE
I *Suggested Answers:* **a)** No, I kept waking up/I woke up several times. **b)** Yes, Don't wake him up - he's very tired. **2 a)** ✔ **b)** Why do you always wake me up when you come home? ... **c)** She was woken up three times during the night...

‚wear 'out; ‚wear sth 'out

to become, or to make something become, thin or no longer able to be used, usually because it has been used too much
CHECK
Meaning: a, d
Grammar: a, b, c, d, f
PRACTISE
I **a)** ...They never seem to wear out. **b)** ..., you'll wear it out. **c)** My son usually grows out of his shoes before he wears them out/they wear out. **d)** ... when the knees wore out. **2 a)** ...because the ones she had were worn out. **b)** Even expensive

trainers wear out... **c)** ...and says he wears out two pairs of shoes a year.

‚wear sb/yourself 'out

to make somebody or yourself extremely tired
CHECK
Meaning: d
Grammar: b, d, f
PRACTISE
I **a)** ...He'll wear himself out. **b)** ...All that shopping has worn me out. **c)** ...Did the journey wear you out? **d)** ...There's no point wearing yourself out. **e)** ...I think the kids have worn him out. **2** *Suggested Answers:* ...I've worn myself out (shopping/digging the garden, etc.) today.

‚work 'out

to happen or develop in a particular way, especially in a successful way
CHECK
Grammar: a
PRACTISE
I **a)** ...but things didn't work out. **b)** ✔ **c)** ✔ **d)** ...Everything worked out really well. **2** *Suggested Answers:* **a)** Fine. It's working out really well. **b)** Unfortunately it isn't working out very well.

‚work sth 'out

to calculate something; to find the answer to a question or something that is difficult to understand or explain
CHECK
Meaning: I b **2** a, c
Grammar: a, b, c, e
PRACTISE
I **a)** It took me a long time to work out the grammar of phrasal verbs. **b)** ✔ **c)** I think it's fun to work out mathematical problems and other puzzles. **2 a)** 15 **b)** a towel

‚write sth 'down

to write something on paper in order to remember or record it
CHECK
Grammar: b, c, d, f
PRACTISE
I **a)** Writing new words down... **b)** ...if it isn't written down. **c)** He's always writing things down in that little book. **2 a)** write **b)** wrote **c)** write it down **d)** write down